FIVE MINUTES
in the
BIBLE
for MEN

BOB BARNES

HARVEST HOUSE PUBLISHERS

EUGENE, OREGON

Cover by e210 Design, Eagon, Minnesota

Cover photo © JSABBOTT / iStockphoto

FIVE MINUTES IN THE BIBLE FOR MEN
Copyright © 2010 by Bob Barnes
Published by Harvest House Publishers
Eugene, Oregon 97402
www.harvesthousepublishers.com

Library of Congress Cataloging-in-Publication Data
Barnes, Bob, 1933-
Five minutes in the Bible for men / Bob Barnes.
   p. cm.
ISBN 978-0-7369-2697-3 (pbk.)
1. Christian men—Prayers and devotions. 2. Bible—Devotional literature. I. Title.
BV4843.B3745 2010
242'.642—dc22
                                        2009017187

10 11 12 13 14 15 16 17 18 / DP-SK / 10 9 8 7 6 5 4 3 2 1

I dedicate this book to the many men who have taken the time to sharpen my iron. They are men who helped me determine my life journey. They have impacted my professional life. Most of them have had a great impact on my spiritual life. They have spent valuable time with me in study and brotherly bonding. I have been privileged having them as friends. They are Art Clausing, Lloyd Arthur, my two brothers, Bill and Kenneth, Del Walker, Bill Beck, Bob Brogger, Roger Garrett, Dr. Craig Merrihew, Jim DeLorenzo, Dave Otto, Bill Whitney, my son Brad, Lloyd Johnson, Hudd Saffell, and many pastors.

I appreciate all of your input into helping me become the man I am today.

—Bob

Introduction

"Iron sharpens iron, so one man sharpens another" (Proverbs 27:17). Yes, other men have an enormous impact upon another man's life. We are not an island unto ourselves. We need other men to come alongside of us to support us when we are down, to help us know of our blind spots, to encourage us when we need encouragement, to hold us accountable when we have asked them to, to give us hard answers when we ask them hard questions. These men are brave enough to tell us when we are going astray or off base. In many cases they are better friends than our own brothers.

This book has been written to help strengthen your daily walk with God. I've attempted to tell you stories that you can relate to—stories that will tug your heartstrings.

It is not easy being a man in the twenty-first century. We are often confused because the world is attempting to make us into men after its own heart and to pull us away from becoming men after God's own heart. May these thoughts affirm to you that you are on the right track—fulfilling what God has desired for your life. After reading these thoughts, I hope that you will be a better husband, father, neighbor, and coworker.

As in my other books, I have placed three boxes (☐ ☐ ☐) in the top section of each devotional so you can check off each devotional after you've read it. This way, you can keep track of what you've read. This system also gives you the freedom to choose readings that fit your need for that day. At the end of each entry I have given you a prayer that relates to the topic, an "action" for you to do that suggests reinforcing the devotional, and a section entitled "Reflections." This space is for you to jot down any thoughts that have come to you during your reading. It can also act as a space to record your journal entries.

May God richly bless you as you read this book. Share it with a friend.

Investing Our Inheritance

May you have the power to understand,
as all God's people should, how wide, how
long, how high, and how deep his love is.
Ephesians 3:18 nlt

In today's culture, a prudent man is recommended to have a will made up stating how he is going to disperse his wealth. Financial planners play a large role in helping people decide how they will maximize their document so their estate doesn't get eaten up by taxes.

However, have you ever thought how you are going to pass on to the next generation your legacy of faith?

The Scriptures are very clear stating the importance of passing on to the next generation what we believe.

- "Remember the days long ago; think about the generations past. Ask your father, and he will inform you. Inquire of your elders, and they will tell you" (Deuteronomy 32:7 nlt).

- "I've also done it so you can tell your children and grand-children...and so you will know that I am the Lord" (Exodus 10:2 nlt).

- "Now that I am old and gray, do not abandon me, O God. Let me proclaim your power to this new generation, your mighty miracles to all who come after me" (Psalm 71:18 nlt).

We as dads need to pass on a few basic truths to the next generation. Our children learn more by watching us than by hearing us. Actions are much more powerful than our words. The "now generation" needs to pass on four basic truths:

1. *Affirm that the Lord is God.*

> "Listen, O Israel! The LORD is our God, the LORD alone" (Deuteronomy 6:4 NLT).

2. *Love the Lord with a whole heart.*

> "You must love the LORD your God with all your heart, all your soul, and all your strength. And you must commit yourselves wholeheartedly to these commands that I am giving you today" (Deuteronomy 6:5-6 NLT).

3. *Teach and train your children.*

> "Repeat them again and again to your children. Talk about them when you are at home and when you are on the road, when you are going to bed and when you are getting up" (Deuteronomy 6:7-9 NLT).

4. *Build a firm foundation.*

> "A house is built by wisdom and becomes strong through good sense. Through knowledge its rooms are filled with all sorts of precious riches and valuables" (Proverbs 24:3-4).

As we live out the Scriptures in our everyday life, our children will soon ask questions regarding our faith in God. These questions will eventually lead to them making their own decision about who God is in their lives.

- "Your children will ask, 'What does this ceremony mean?'" (Exodus 12:26 NLT).
- "In the future, your children will ask you, 'What does this all mean?'" (Exodus 13:14 NLT).
- "We will use these stones to build a memorial. In the future your children will ask you, 'What do these stones mean?'" (Joshua 4:6 NLT).

In Psalm 78:4-6 the psalmist tells us men not to hide these truths from our children. We are to tell the next generation about our Lord—about His power—about His mighty wonders. We are commanded to teach them to our children, so that the next generation might know them. We are to pass the story down from generation to generation.

———⁓⁓⁓———

PRAYER: Father God, let me grasp this responsibility to pass on my godly truths to my children who in turn can pass it on to their children. Let them see Christ in my life. Amen.

ACTION: Live life on purpose. Stop shooting from the hip. You'll never hit your target if you don't have a plan.

REFLECTIONS

We Are Seasoners of Life

You are the salt of the earth.
MATTHEW 5:13

One of my favorite TV programs is *Emeril Live*. Emeril Lagasse is a very charismatic chef from New Orleans. In his food preparation, he is always talking about seasoning and taking it "up a notch." When he throws in the seasoning he gives a very active arm and hand motion and utters a high-pitched "BAM!" as the seasoning hits the food.

For Emeril, seasoning food is huge. And his fans love his theatrics, letting out an enthusiastic cheer when he takes it "up a notch" and utters his classic "BAM!" They all know that food without seasoning is bland and less appealing to the fine diner.

That's the way it is in our Christian life too. If we are bland and have no flavor, no one will want to follow our recipe for life. Jesus tells us that we are to be the salt of the earth. We are to be seasoners of life to all those we meet in this decaying world.

Some time ago, before Hurricane Katrina hit New Orleans in 2005, Emilie and I spent five days in New Orleans. After seeing Bourbon Street in the French Quarter—a section of town only tourists visit—we agreed this area represented the dark and decaying elements of life well. It was just this sort of decay and decadence that Jesus saved us from. As we saw the darkness there, we both said, "Thank You, Jesus, for what You did on the cross for us."

There is a difference between Christ-followers and the world:

11

> We all, with unveiled face, beholding as in a mirror the glory
> of the Lord, are being transformed into the same image from
> glory to glory, just as from the Lord, the Spirit.
>
> —2 Corinthians 3:18 nasb

As believers, our faces reflect the Spirit of the Lord. Our character is often the only Bible the unbeliever will ever read. Our countenance radiates that there is something different about us. Many times people will ask us, "Are you a Christian?" When we say "yes," they will reply, "I thought so—you seem to have a calmness the rest of the world doesn't have!"

Our call as Christian men is twofold:

- We are to stand against moral decay and darkness.
- We bring light and seasoning to the outside world.

Throughout Scripture Jesus shares that we are to be influencers of the world (rather than being influenced by the world).

- "Jesus again spoke to them, saying, 'I am the Light of the world; he who follows Me will not walk in the darkness, but will have the Light of life'" (John 8:12 nasb).

- "Let your light shine before men in such a way that they may see your works, and glorify your Father who is in heaven" (Matthew 5:16 nasb).

- "In everything...treat people the same way you want them to treat you, for this is the Law and the Prophets" (Matthew 7:12 nasb).

- "The whole Law is fulfilled in one word, in the statement, 'You shall love your neighbor as yourself'" (Galatians 5:14 nasb).

As seasoners of life, let's be reminded that one of our main purposes is to love, love, and love. Each time we shed light upon a family member, a neighbor, or a fellow worker we are showering God's love upon them. Whenever our lives reflect the love of God, our heavenly Father is glorified.

—◦◦◦—

PRAYER: Father God, thank You for impressing on me the importance of being a seasoner to those I come into contact with each day. I so want to reflect Your love to them. Continue to remind me I am the light and salt of the world. Amen.

ACTION: Each time you pick up the salt and pepper shakers to season your food, may you be reminded that you are a seasoner of life.

REFLECTIONS

Never Give Up

We never give up. Though our bodies are dying, our
inner strength in the Lord is growing every day.
2 CORINTHIANS 4:16 TLB

I love to see the underdog hang in there and never give up. Some of the great comebacks in sports are about teams who didn't have a chance to be victorious before the game began, or the team who was predicted to win, but by the middle of the game they were losing. Then something happens—the underdogs come on strong in the second half of the game and at the last minute they claim victory.

Yogi Berra, the famous catcher and Hall of Famer for the New York Yankees, had a famous saying, "It's not over 'til it's over."

One of the great principles of growing in the Lord is to keep growing each day. A little by little and precept by precept. The tortoise beat the hare by slowly but consistently not giving up.

If you have financial troubles, setbacks…it's not the end.

If you have been lied to and deceived…it's not the end.

If you have lost your job…it's not the end.

If you have lost your home…it's not the end.

If something has been stolen from you or if you have been robbed of your inheritance…it's not the end.

If you have a child who is ensnared in sin, entangled in a web of wrong relationships, failing according to life's report card, or refusing to communicate with you…it's not the end.

If your mate has walked away, chosen someone else instead of you…it's not the end.

If you have just lost a loved one to death—sudden death, expected or unexpected—it's not the end. Even if your loved one committed suicide…it's not the end.

If you are incarcerated for a crime…it's not the end.

If you are losing your hearing or your sight…it's not the end.

If you are in the depths of depression, if you are battling depression or a chemical imbalance that has thrown all your emotions and even your way of doing things out of kilter…it's not the end.

If you have learned that you have a terminal disease, a crippling disease, a wasting disease…it's not the end.

If you have stepped onto the threshold of death…it's not the end.

I can tell you all this with the utmost of confidence and know that what I am telling you is truth.

It may seem like the end…

You may wish it were the end…

But it is not the end because God is God and the end has not yet come.[1]

—⁓—

PRAYER: Father God, thank You again for assuring me this isn't the end, for the end will be an "eternal weight of glory" far beyond all comparison. I trust You for perfecting what's taking place in my life. Amen.

ACTION: In your journal, list several of your temporary afflictions. Beside each one, write, "This is producing an eternal weight of glory for me."

Reflections

What Is Your Safety Net?

Remember your Creator in the days of your youth.
ECCLESIASTES 12:1

Many of us depend upon our money, jobs, other people, or material things to make us happy and to bail us out of tough times. Others become dependent on drugs or alcohol to ease the pain of life. We all depend upon something to seemingly make us happy, if for only a short time.

My question is, "Why not depend on the only One who can give us eternal, abundant life and true satisfaction?"

Even in Solomon's day they were trying to find fun, amusement, pleasure, knowledge, security, and love. They had the same quest for happiness that we do today.

It is recorded in Ecclesiastes 1:2: "Vanity of vanities, all is vanity." Here's the bottom line of what this verse is saying: "It's all just a bubble that bursts." Solomon was the Warren Buffett and the Bill Gates of his day. He had it all plus more. He had more material possessions than perhaps any other man in history. At the end of his life, Solomon said, "Remember your Creator in the days of your youth" (Ecclesiastes 12:1).

Solomon's wisdom excelled the wisdom of all the men of the East and all the wisdom of Egypt. He set his heart to know wisdom and to know madness and folly. He perceived that this was like grasping for the wind. It's all a bubble that bursts.

Even with all of Solomon's wisdom, his mind could not bring him to salvation. Yes, our minds are very important, but we cannot think our way to God. We come by faith, and then our mind will support our faith.

By grace you have been saved through faith; and that not of yourselves, it is the gift of God; not as a result of works, that no one may boast.

—EPHESIANS 2:8-9 NASB

Solomon had every pleasure—everything at the snap of his fingers. He had 700 wives and 300 concubines, hundreds of servants, and every exotic food from around the world. He could afford every sensual pleasure that one could imagine. Yet in the end, he said, "It's all a bubble that bursts. It doesn't satisfy."

Men, what is our safety net to save us when we fall? If Solomon says that it doesn't satisfy, what makes us think that we can find satisfaction in life without knowing God through Jesus Christ. We must step off the throne and place God on top. He is the only one that has eternal satisfaction. Paul says in Romans 1:16: "I am not ashamed of the gospel, for it is the power of God for salvation to everyone who believes, to the Jew first and also to the Greek" (NASB).

When we live this kind of life, we will have joy, happiness, and satisfaction. Let's admit that our bubble will burst someday—where will we go for safety?

—∿∿—

PRAYER: Father God, help me to realize that all of my wealth, my toys, my stock portfolio will someday go up in smoke. Let me rest knowing that You are my shield and my protector. Amen.

ACTION: Put your faith into action. Make some eternal changes in your life.

REFLECTIONS

The Benefits of a Kite String

The righteous will live by faith.
GALATIANS 3:11

When the first suspension bridge across the Niagara River was to be erected, the question was how to get the cable across the river. With the favoring wind, a kite was sent aloft, which soon landed on the other shore. To its thin string a larger cord was attached, which was drawn over the river—then a rope, then a larger rope, then a cable strong enough to support the iron cable, which in turn supported the bridge.

All of this could never have been done without the thin kite string. Even so, a weak faith reaches to Christ and heaven, and may enlarge to gigantic proportions, holding its possessor securely anchored in their belief system.

That's the way we are in life. Our faith starts out as an insignificant string and then develops into a cord, then a rope, then a large rope, and finally a cable.

> Faith is not belief without proof, but trust without reservations.
>
> —ELTON TRUEBLOOD

In our world of comparisons, we want to start out right away as a cable because that's what we see around us. But always remember that those cables started out as insignificant kite strings and have developed and grown over the years into that cable you so greatly admire today.

Spiritual growth results from trusting in God the Father, God the Son, and God the Holy Spirit. In today's key verse, we see that the righteous man lives by faith. That faith must have an object, and for the Christian, that object is Jesus Christ. He has given Himself to us as believers to atone for our sins; through Him we have forgiveness of those sins and a direct line to God the Father.

A life of faith will enable you to trust God increasingly with every detail of your life, and to practice the following:

G—Go to God in daily prayer (John 15:7).

R—Read God's Word daily (Acts 17:11).

Begin with the Gospel of John.

O—Obey God moment by moment (John 14:21).

W—Witness for Christ by your life and words (John 15:8).

T—Trust God for every detail of your life (1 Peter 5:7).

H—Holy Spirit: Allow Him to control and empower your daily life and witness (Galatians 5:16-17; Acts 1:8).

Growth as a Christian is a matter of choice. Each day you must make the crucial decision again: Am I going to follow Jesus today? Each day you must gather from your soul, "Yes, I am going to follow Jesus today!" You might be thinking, "Do I have to make this same decision every day for the rest of my life?" My answer to you is, "Yes, you have to make this same fundamental decision each day. The fruits and blessings of today are based upon the decisions you made yesterday. Success generally doesn't come by accident."

—◦◦◦—

PRAYER: Father God, let me be willing to start out with a kite string before I become a cable. I must work through the process of growing in my faith. Amen.

ACTION: Develop a plan and let the plan work for you.

REFLECTIONS

Our Father Who Art in Heaven

Our Father which art in heaven...
MATTHEW 6:9 KJV

This wonderful model of prayer begins with this adoration of God: *Our Father which art in heaven...*

God tenderly invites us to believe that He is truly our Father, and we are truly His children, so we may ask of Him in all cheerfulness and confidence, as dear children ask of their dear father. James 4:2 states, "You do not have, because you do not ask God." As any loving Father, God wants us to boldly approach His throne and commit our requests, our adoration, our thanks, and supplications to Him in the form of prayer.

E.M. Bounds expressed it so simply when he wrote:

> God is always within call it is true; His ear is ever attentive to the cry of His child, but we can never get to know Him if we use the vehicle of prayer as we use the telephone—for a few words of hurried conversation. Intimacy requires development. We can never know God as it is our privilege to know Him by brief repetitions that are requests of personal favors and nothing more. That is not the way in which we can come into communication with heaven's King. We try many ways to cope with the many stresses of life. Often we escape into work, leisure time, body toning, and exercise, and even many kinds of addictions. Often these escapes look like a way to survive, but behaviors turned to as responses to stress—even those with religious trappings—are

not the solution. God Himself is the only one who can direct us to live life as He meant it to be.

Because God is so near to us, we can approach Him in a very personal way. When we open our prayer with the phrase, "Our Father," we acknowledge that the answers of life lie beyond our abilities, our looks, our social position, and our economic status.

We admit that our might is not enough to live the fullest life that God intended for us. We have to be very brave to admit we need someone bigger than we are. But we can call upon the Father in confidence, knowing that we are His children and that He hears us.

We gain strength and confidence when we call on God by name and admit that we need Him for our every need and that we are helpless without Him.[2]

As men, one of the most difficult recognitions is that we need help from someone greater than we are. Our culture has taught us well (but in error) that we are capable to control our own destiny. Only when we humble ourselves can we truly understand what this life is all about. Don't wait until you are in a moment of stress that your heart turns heavenly. Prepare yourself first, then face your disappointments. Only then will you be able to cope with the pitfalls of life.

—⟨⟩—

PRAYER: Father God, give me the courage to trust in You for all that life will toss at me. I want to be ready and prepared to face these difficulties as I meet them. Amen.

ACTION: Begin a daily routine of reading God's Word each day. Store it in your heart for that rainy day.

REFLECTIONS

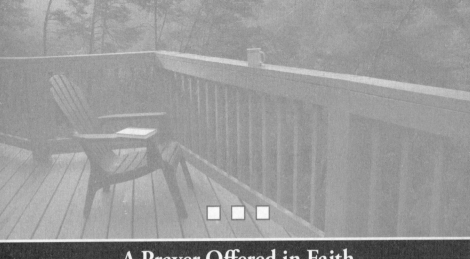

A Prayer Offered in Faith

*Is anyone among you sick? Then he must call for the
elders of the church and they are to pray over him,
anointing him with oil in the name of the Lord.*
JAMES 5:14 NASB

In this passage God may heal directly, through medicine, or in answer to prayer. The oil is a symbol of the presence of God.

- "Thou preparest a table before me in the presence of mine enemies: thou anointest my head with oil" (Psalm 23:5 KJV).

- "[He] came to him and bandaged up his wounds, pouring oil and wine on them" (Luke 10:34 NASB).

  Prayers of faith are answered not simply because they are prayed in faith, but only if they are prayed in the will of God.

- "If we ask anything according to His will, He hears us" (1 John 5:14 NASB).

God does not always think it best to heal. Paul had a thorn in the flesh which he prayed would be removed. However, the Lord said to Paul, "My grace is sufficient for you, for power is perfected in weakness." Paul replied, "Most gladly, therefore, I will rather boast about my weaknesses, so that the power of Christ may dwell in me. Therefore I am well content with weaknesses, with insults, with distresses, with persecution, with difficulties, for Christ's sake; for when I am weak, then I am strong" (2 Corinthians 12:8-10 NASB).

> In the morning, prayer is the key that opens to us the treasures of God's mercies and blessings; in the evening, it is the key that shuts us up under His protection and safeguard.
>
> —UNKNOWN

When Emilie was first diagnosed with cancer, I went to the elders of the church and asked them to pray and anoint her with oil as James 5:14 taught. It was a beautiful ceremony. She had never been anointed with oil before, so we didn't know what to expect. We were desiring for immediate and complete healing. When she wasn't immediately healed, we felt somewhat disappointed and were let down temporarily—not wanting to accept the fact that God said, "Not yet." It wasn't until many months later that we could see and feel the effects of her healing taking place.

Emilie and I had come to agreement that we could and would be content with God's will for our lives. Even like Job when his wife told him to curse God and die, he replied, "Shall we indeed accept good from God and not accept adversity?" (Job 2:10 NASB).

> Prayer doesn't get man's will done in heaven; it gets God's will done on earth.
>
> —RONALD DUNN

———

PRAYER: Father God, I thank You for Your provision, that we are to seek out the elders of our church and ask them to pray and anoint us with oil. It makes us depend upon Your will for us. Amen.

ACTION: Have a great faith today as you lift up a prayer to God.

REFLECTIONS

No One Likes Bad News

Light arises in the darkness for the upright...
PSALM 112:4 NASB

When we hear the phone ring at 2:00 AM, or a friend is ill and we are anxiously waiting beside the phone to hear the latest report, our heart skips a beat and races faster than usual. Why? Because we expect to hear bad news. It could be good or bad, but our human nature leads us to think the worst.

As humans, we seem to fear bad news. It may be a natural concern for the safety of others, but it can be just the dread of hearing the worst. Confidence in God helps us overcome the dread of bad news.

- "Praise the LORD! How blessed is the man who fears the LORD, who greatly delights in His commandments" (Psalm 112:1 NASB).

- "He will not fear evil tidings; his heart is steadfast, trusting in the LORD" (Psalm 112:7 NASB).

When the heartbeat of fear enters our body, we need to go to Scripture to find those verses that give us comfort.

The Bible doesn't promise that we will never receive bad news. But it does assure us that we don't have to live each day in agonizing fear of what might happen.

A hymn by Frances Havergal reminds us that a trusting heart is the answer for a worried mind.

Stayed upon Jehovah, hearts are fully blest;
Finding, as He promised, perfect peace and rest.

—FRANCES RIDLEY HAVERGAL

—∾∾—

PRAYER: Father God, may I not fear when the phone rings at odd hours. Let my heart hear Your words that give comfort. Amen.

ACTION: Eighty-five percent of the things you worry about never happen. Trust God's promises.

REFLECTIONS

Take Time to Care

Rejoice with those who rejoice, and weep with those who weep.
ROMANS 12:15 NASB

Being used by God to minister to others is one of the greatest privileges of a believer, and He's equipped you with all you need. You only have to be willing and sensitive to His leading.

One of the great benefits of having cancer is that you have the opportunity to share your hope with those who seemingly have no hope. While in Seattle with Emilie awaiting a bone marrow transplant, we had many opportunities to rejoice when a fellow patient got good news and we also wept many times when the patient received bad news.

One couple in particular gave us an opportunity to do both. They were young, successful, energetic, and both very professional in their careers. They came from the east coast and were a long way from friends and family. We gave them great comfort while in the hospital.

As we often did, we wrote out selected psalms on three-by-five cards and slipped them under various patients' apartment doors. One morning as we were placing a card under the door the door swung open—we were caught. Marshall's wife said, "Come in. I want to show you what we are doing with your cards." She walked us into the kitchen and showed us all the previous cards pasted on the kitchen cabinet doors. She said, "Don't stop putting the cards under our door. We love them, and they give us inspiration and hope." She went on to tell us that Marshall's mother was coming to town the next weekend and wanted to know if we could come and pray for Marshall.

We did, and it was a wonderful experience. We prayed for both Emilie and Marshall and I had the privilege to anoint both with oil in accordance with James 5. That Sunday afternoon we rejoiced and shed tears at the same time.

Through this experience we were able to become very good friends over the following months. There came a call one evening that Marshall had contracted an infection and had to be transported by ambulance to the University of Washington's Medical Hospital.

On the eventful Sunday when we had prayed with Marshall, I had shared John 3:16 as part of the promises that Scripture gives us as believers. On several occasions Marshall's wife kept telling me that Marshall had a story to tell me—but on each occasion something seemed to be more important.

As soon as we heard that Marshall was in the hospital, we took a shuttle up to the hospital to visit him. Upon arrival to his bedside, he had several members of his family with him. He was preoccupied by the urgency of the moment. Upon returning back to our place of residence, I expressed to Emilie that I prayed that I would have one more day with Marshall before he died—as I wasn't sure that Marshall knew Jesus as his Savior.

The Lord honored my request. Therefore, we went to visit him the next day. This time no one was in the room but Marshall and myself. Emilie and his mom went down to the chapel to pray. Marshall was breathing heavy, and his face was covered with a large oxygen mask. We greeted each other. I sat on the side of the bed, leaning over to hear his faint words. In a low tone, he said, "Bob, I have a story to tell you. When I was a young boy, I would visit my grandfather on his farm in Georgia every summer. During my stay, he would make me memorize Scripture verses. One of them was John 3:16. I never knew what it meant until that Sunday you came to pray for me, and you broke it apart, word by word. I finally understood what it meant."

This gave me an opportunity to ask Marshall if he believed that God sent His Son, Jesus, to earth to die for our sins, and that if we believed in Jesus we would have everlasting life. Marshall nodded yes, and I responded, "Based on your profession in Jesus as your personal Savior, you will be saved and live with Him forever in heaven." Needless to say, we had rejoicing and tears in our eyes.

I could see that Marshall was tired. I gave a short prayer confirming Marshall's testimony and excused myself from his hospital room. I journeyed down to the chapel to tell Emilie and his mom the good news. They too rejoiced and had tears.

Emilie and I again went back to our apartment. The next morning at about 8:00 AM, our phone rang, and Marshall's mom was on the other end. She announced to us that Marshall had gone to be with the Lord in the middle of the night.

Again we were able to rejoice and shed tears. I was so glad that God had given me one more day to be with Marshall.

Remember, you have the Holy Spirit. His ministry is to guide you into all truth (John 16:13), to bring to your remembrance the truths you've learned. God's truth sets people free. When you minister, ask the Holy Spirit to show you what truths the person needs.

Being used by God to minister to others is one of the greatest privileges of a believer. He's equipped you with all you need. You only have to be willing and sensitive to His leading.

> God so loved the world, that He gave His only begotten Son, that whoever believes in Him should not perish, but have eternal life.
>
> —John 3:16 NASB

PRAYER: Father God, may we as believers be able to rejoice and to shed tears with those who need them. Amen.

ACTION: Share a joyful thought and/or a tear today with someone who needs that—maybe even a stranger.

REFLECTIONS

Make Love Without Doing It

Your two breasts are like two fawns.
SOLOMON 4:5

For some reason, our marketers in print media and advertising executives try to portray sex as something that is fashionable, and everyone's doing it. I remember a quote from Billy Graham. The reporter wanted to know how he and Ruth had romance in the elder years. His reply was very touching. "Ruth and I romance with our eyes." Isn't that true? The older you get, the more you realize there are a lot of ways to make love without doing it. Emilie and I often just sit on the sofa and hold hands, or we walk on the beach holding hands, or we hide a love note under each other's pillow.

A man often comes into the bedroom and leans up against the doorsill and announces to his wife, "Tonight's the night." After a long hard day with the children—cooking meals and cleaning the home—she answers back, "For what?"

We men need to know that our wives look at sex differently than we do. Below you will find several ideas for you to consider when your wife answers, "For what?"

- Hold hands.
- Give a big hug.
- Respect each other.
- Give each other sexy looks.
- Write a poem for her.

- Send her flowers.
- Rent a romantic video.
- Listen to music together.
- Take a scenic drive.
- Flirt with each other.
- Trust one another.
- Talk on the telephone.
- Wash her car.
- Listen to her hurts.
- Be faithful.
- Help her with the housework.
- Send her a funny card.
- Tell her a funny joke.
- Make a list of what you like about her. Give it to her.
- Give her a special gift.
- Take her out to a nice restaurant.
- Read a book together.
- Visit a museum.
- Relax in a spa.
- Give her a gift certificate to her favorite store.
- Take a bike ride, and remember to wear a helmet.
- Take a walk arm-in-arm together.

If you follow these 27 ideas, your wife won't answer you with "For what?" as often.

> Love isn't like a reservoir. You'll never drain it dry. It's much more like a natural spring. The longer and the farther it flows, the stronger and the deeper and the clearer it becomes.
>
> —Eddie Cantor

PRAYER: Father God, let me broaden my idea about sex. I want to be sensitive to my wife's moods and energy level. I want her to enjoy our romance as much as I do. Amen.

ACTION: Pick out one of these 27 ideas and do it today.

REFLECTIONS

The Same Yesterday and Today

Even children are known by the way they act, whether their
conduct is pure and right. Children who mistreat their father or
chase away their mother are a public disgrace and embarrassment.
PROVERBS 20:11; 19:26 NLT

As I journey to our local mall and sees the conduct of the teenagers I wonder, "What is this world coming to?" Even scanning the TV sitcoms, we see the dumbing down of the next generation. As I get older I find a wider generation gap between my values and those that are portrayed in today's culture.

I don't understand their music, their choice of clothing, their manners, and their frequent disrespect for adult and authority figures.

A 6,000-year-old Egyptian tomb bears this inscription: "We live in a decadent age. Young people no longer respect their parents. They are rude and impatient. They inhabit taverns and have no self-control."

The next time you think the "modern generation" is going from bad to worse, remember that God always has a rich handful of teen heroes ready to change the world. In Bible times, the heroes were Joseph the dreamer, Daniel in Babylon, David the giant-killer, and the virgin Mary (likely still a teen when the angel visited her).

As a teenager, Charles Spurgeon preached to great crowds, but when they referred to his youthfulness, he replied, "Never mind my age. Think of the Lord Jesus Christ and His preciousness."

In our own day, we've been deeply moved by young people like 17-year-old Cassie Bernall of Littleton, Colorado, who was shot for her faith during the Columbine tragedy.

Some of our greatest hymns were also written by young adults. Isaac Watts wrote most of his memorable hymns at about the age of 19. When poet John Milton was 15 he wrote the well-known hymn "Let Us with a Gladsome Mind." The hymn "Work for the Night Is Coming" was written by an 18-year-old. And "My Jesus, I Love Thee"—a hymn of deep devotion—was written by William Ralph Featherston at age 16. Sixteen!

Featherston was born July 23, 1846, in Montreal. He died in the same city 26 years later. His family attended the Wesleyan Methodist Church, and it seems likely that William wrote this hymn as a poem celebrating his conversion to Christ. Reportedly, he sent it to an aunt living in California, and somehow it was published anonymously in a British hymnal in 1864.

Little else is known about the origin of the hymn or its author, but that's all right. It's enough just to know that God can change the world through anyone—regardless of age—who will say, "My Jesus, I love Thee, I know Thou art mine. For Thee, all the follies of sin I resign."[3]

Yes, from the beginning of time we have had adults who viewed their youth with not having the capability of continuing our culture. However, we are excited when we read in the newspaper, see on TV, or personally experience in our own lives the great stories about our young people. They are brighter and better-educated than ever before. They have technological skills and understanding that we often don't comprehend. My grandchildren are the ones I go to when I have a question regarding my electronic equipment.

It is our responsibility as adults to teach them to have spiritual values as they carry the next generation forward.

Children have more need of models than of critics.

—JOSEPH JOUBERT

———

PRAYER: Father God, give me the patience to see good in what
           I can't understand. Let me do my part in preparing
           my children for the next generation. Amen.

ACTION: Share one bit of wisdom with your children today. Get
           some ideas from the book of Proverbs.

REFLECTIONS

Take Time to Read the Book

All Scripture is God-breathed and is useful for teaching, rebuking, correcting and training in righteousness.
2 TIMOTHY 3:16

In 1835, Harvard scholar Richard Henry Dana took time off from his studies and went to sea for his health. It almost broke him. From his experiences, he wrote *Two Years Before the Mast*, the first account of life at sea written from the perspective of a common seaman.

It was a very hard life—often dangerous, usually uncomfortable, the food unchanging, and human contact sparse. Working the West Coast collecting hides (for shoes in the East), Dana wrote, "Here we were, in a little vessel, with a small crew, on a half-civilized coast, at the ends of the earth…" He was in Santa Barbara, California.

To make matters worse, the captain was tyrannical. Punishing a small infraction with brutal whipping was not beyond him. On ship there was no other law, no redress, no way out. It was these kinds of experiences that caused Dana to vow, were he ever to get back to America (California was still part of Mexico), that he would dedicate himself to lighten the sufferings of this poor class of people, one of which he had become.

In fact, that is what happened. Dana later took up maritime law and brought about some significant changes.

Since then, Dana has been pretty much forgotten. There's a town by his name along the California coast (Dana Point) with his statue, a replica of his ship, and curiosities for tourists. But if people haven't read his book, they don't know his story—and most haven't.

In a way there's a parallel between what Dana did for seamen and what the Lord did for us all. He came and identified with the poor, working, and suffering. He dedicated himself to the solution of our pains. In the years since then statues have been erected and memorabilia have been sold, but a great many people still don't know much about our Lord. Most haven't read His book.[4]

As men, it is very important that we establish a time where we can individually get into God's Word and see what He has for us in it.

Sometimes we have insurance, credit cards, and membership policies that grant us privileges we know nothing about because we haven't taken the time to read all the benefits we have through being a member in good standing of a certain organization. That's the way it is with the Bible. We miss out on some great blessings because we haven't taken the time to read the Book.

Here are a few blessings you might have missed:

- "God so loved the world that he gave his one and only Son, that whoever believes in him shall not perish but have eternal life" (John 3:16).

- "To all who received him, to those who believed in his name, he gave the right to become children of God" (John 1:12).

- "He who is kind to the poor lends to the Lord, and he will reward him for what he has done" (Proverbs 19:17).

- "He gives strength to the weary and increases the power of the weak" (Isaiah 40:29).

- "The fruit of the Spirit is love, joy, peace, patience, kindness, goodness, faithfulness, gentleness and self-control" (Galatians 5:22).

- "The fear of the LORD adds length to life, but the years of the wicked are cut short" (Proverbs 10:27).

Don't let another day go by in your Christian walk without taking the time to discover at least one new promise for the day. A good beginning is reading the books of Psalms and Proverbs. Each verse you will want to have engraved on your brain, for each is inspirational. Many of them appear on plaques and greeting cards. You may say, "I've read that before, but I didn't realize it came from the Bible."

PRAYER: Father God, give me a thirst to read the Book. I have good intentions but I have a hard time getting started. Amen.

ACTION: Start reading the book of Proverbs today. There are 31 chapters—read the one appropriate for the day of the month.

REFLECTIONS

Seven Things God Hates

The fear of the LORD is the beginning of knowledge, but fools despise wisdom and discipline.
PROVERBS 1:7

It seems like men always ask the quantitative question, "How much do I have to do to be a good Christian?" We know that God is a loving God, but He is also one that hates certain things. King Solomon was well aware of that when in the book of Proverbs he listed seven things God hates.

We can be assured that if Solomon, the world's wisest man, lists them, that he felt they were important enough to be passed down to us men in the twenty-first century.

Here are those seven things God hates (Proverbs 6:16-19):

1. Haughty eyes.

2. A lying tongue.

3. Hands that shed innocent blood.

4. A heart that devises wicked plans.

5. Feet that run rapidly to evil.

6. A false witness who utters lies.

7. One who spreads strife among brothers.

Each of these abominations deal with character flaws of an unwise man. They are the manifestations of fools who have not been willing to hear and learn from authority figures like parents, teachers, coaches, law enforcement officers, and military officers. They may have heard when they were young, but they decided early in life they wanted to short-circuit the system—they had to have fun now, because tomorrow might never come.

How about you? Do any of these warnings occur in your life? Did one strike you as you read the list? You may reflect on the "old" you who used to do these things—I used to do that, but not anymore. God has given me a new heart. I am a new man—old things have passed away, and now I am a changed man.

When Solomon is so impressed by God's hatred for this list of seven, he wants to warn us with a big red flag that says, "Pay attention—these seven things will give you death, not life." He gives an urgent call!

> Truly, truly, I say to you, he who hears my word; and believes Him who sent Me, has eternal life, and does not come into judgment, but has passed out of death into life.
>
> —JOHN 5:24 NASB

God has given each man the capacity to decide upon our destiny. The believer says, "God, Thy will be done," and God says to the unbeliever, "Your will be done." In both cases, we will live in eternity by what decision we make regarding what kind of man we want to be. You decide—it's your destiny.

———

PRAYER: Father God, may I be wise enough to accept on faith that Jesus is who the Bible says He is. I certainly want to choose life over death. Amen.

ACTION: Take and analyze each of the seven abominations that are listed. What changes in your life, if any, need to be made?

REFLECTIONS

How Much for a Whistle?

Esau...sold his own birthright for a single meal.
HEBREWS 12:16 NASB

Have you ever laughed at someone who paid a ridiculous price for an antique, a vintage car, a boat, or an outdoor barbecue? I sometimes look in travel magazines and see where they are advertising a week's vacation in Hawaii for a thousand dollars a night. I say to myself, "Who in their right mind would pay that much for a place to sleep?"

One of our great Americans, Ben Franklin, tells a little story about a whistle. It brings home the common sense of not selling one's birthright. You've often heard that "common sense" is not so common anymore—and how true that is.

When Ben was only seven years old, he was charmed by the whistle of a friend and impetuously traded all the pennies he had to his friend for this noisemaker. His purchase made him the target of his family and friends, who pointed out to him the folly of bargaining before reflecting on the worth of one's purchase.

> Experience is a wonderful thing. It enables you to recognize a
> mistake when you make it again.
>
> —FRANKLIN P. JONES

In our lives, we run across a lot of whistles for sale. Our "common sense" question is, "Are we paying too much for the whistle?" This is especially true when it comes to trading our reputation for a trinket. If former President

Clinton had asked himself this question, he might have realized that the price of the whistle named Monica Lewinsky was too much, and he would not have chosen to pay the price he did.

> Our strength is shown in the things we stand for;
> Our weakness is shown in the things we fall for.
>
> —UNKNOWN

Another woman has a husband who travels a lot and she has become bored with her lifestyle. A very nice gentleman friend helped her break up her boredom by taking her out to dinner and to the theater. What had been a casual occasion has now become a regular occurrence. Is she paying too much for the whistle?

What is a whistle worth? As Christian men, we must use the Word of God to help us determine the value of the whistles in our lives. Many times we must answer, "That whistle isn't worth the asking price."

—⁓⁓—

PRAYER: Father God, when we find ourselves looking to the future because we aren't content with today, may You give me a peace of mind that lets us rest where You have placed us. Amen.

ACTION: Tell the story of Ben Franklin's whistle to your children at dinner tonight. After you share a time when you paid too much for a whistle, ask them if they can think of a time when they have done the same.

REFLECTIONS

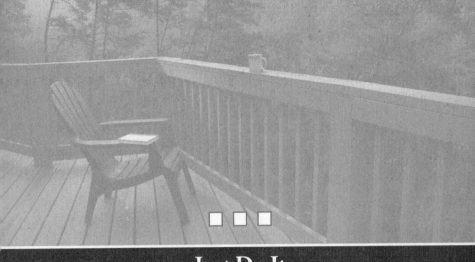

Just Do It

I can do all things through Christ which strengtheneth me.
PHILIPPIANS 4:13 KJV

One of the great advertising slogans is that given by Nike, the leading manufacturer of sports shoes in the world. We all have seen it in their media commercials—"Just do it." They're three simple words, but they powerfully suggest that we should get out of bed or off that couch and put our dreams into action.

The first step is halfway to your destination.

Many years ago, my telephone rang. I picked up the receiver and heard these words: "PaPa, what is that verse of Scripture that says, 'I can do all things through Christ which gives me strength'?"

"Oh, Chad, that is one of my favorite verses. Look up Philippians 4:13." The phone went silent for a few minutes and on comes Chad who was about 12 years old and in the sixth grade. I asked him why he wanted to know about that particular verse of Scripture. He replied, "I'm in a race at school tomorrow, and I'm so nervous that I can't relax, and I needed that verse to give me added strength when I pray. Thanks, PaPa."

I told him I would pray for him tomorrow, and I asked him to call me back and let me know how he did.

Well, by 4:00 PM the next day, the phone rang, and it was Chad on the other end. I knew by the excitement of his voice that he had done well. I asked, "Chad, how did you do?"

"PaPa, you won't believe it, but I won and set a new school record for that event. I've never done so well. Thank you for your prayers and helping me find the verse."

That verse will be etched in Chad's memory. He will always be able to find that verse and he will recall it whenever he needs extra strength for any situation in life. Yes, we can do all things through Christ who strengthens us. How can I be so sure? Because the Scriptures give us that promise and God never goes back on what He has promised.

The next time you come to a fork in the road, just remember—"Just do it."

> He who believes is strong; he who doubts is weak. Strong convictions precede great actions.
>
> —J.F. Clarke

PRAYER: Father God, You truly give me added strength by all Your promises. I'm so encouraged by Your Word. Amen.

ACTION: Pray today with the simple and unshakable faith of a child.

REFLECTIONS

Who Is Going to Bell the Cat?

Be strong and courageous! Do not tremble or be dismayed,
for the LORD your God is with you wherever you go.
JOSHUA 1:9 NASB

Consider this fable:

> Once upon a time all the mice met together in council and discussed the best means of protecting themselves against the attacks of the cat. After several suggestions had been debated, a mouse of some standing and experience got up and said, "I think I have hit upon a plan which ensures our safety in the future, provided you approve and carry it out. It is that we should fasten a bell around the neck of our enemy the cat, which will by its tinkling warn us of her approach."
>
> This proposal was warmly applauded, and it had already been decided to adopt it when an old mouse finally got up on his feet and said, "I agree with you all that the plan before us is an admirable one, but I ask: Who is going to bell the cat?"[5]

Men in America have become feminized over the last 20 or more years. We have lost the masculine touch. Look at our dress, our hairstyles, our softness, our passivity. Where have all the real men gone?

Wouldn't it be wonderful if all we had to do in order to be brave is to talk about it? But true courage and bravery require action. Our society today hungers to find men with courage. We look for our heroes in sports, politics, movies, business, and church, but many of them fail the test. We hunger for the character trait of courage in our men, but few are able to deliver it.

As parents we are continually tested by the decisions we must make. Are we able to stand alone and make hard decisions on what our family is going to do? It's hard to be in the minority as a friend, a neighbor, or a parent, to just say "no." Unfortunately, the greatest pressure often comes from those we love the most!

In Joshua 24:15, the writer had a similar dilemma, but he stood tall and delivered this statement:

> If it is disagreeable in your sight to serve the LORD, choose for yourselves today whom you will serve: whether the gods which your fathers served which were beyond the river, or the gods of the Amorites in whose land you are living; but as for me and my house, we will serve the LORD (NASB).

Joshua was willing to stand up and be heard. He had the courage to bell the cat. Are you facing a similar difficulty in your life? If so, look to God to find the answer. He says He will never leave us or forsake us. That is a promise we can take to the bank.

> The world has no room for cowards. We must all be ready somehow to toil, to suffer, to die. And yours is not the less noble because no drum beats before you when you go out to your daily battlefields, and no crowds shout your coming when you return from your daily victory and defeat.
>
> —ROBERT LOUIS STEVENSON

—◦◦◦—

PRAYER: Father God, make me a man of courage. Let me have the strength to be a man after your own heart. I want to be a brave warrior for what's good and honorable. Amen.

ACTION: Put a bell on a cat today.

REFLECTIONS

Is Not This the Carpenter?

Is not this the carpenter, the son of Mary, and brother
of James and Joses and Judas and Simon?
MARK 6:3 NASB

If you're like me, you have an image in your mind of what Jesus may have looked like. I know we've all seen the many famous renditions of Jesus' portrait, but did He really look like that? How dark was His skin? How tall was He? Did He really have long hair and a beard? If Jesus would appear today, would we recognize Him? Was He media-handsome, which some think necessary to be accepted today? How would He have looked on TV? Did He have a strong masculine speaking voice?

All these questions appear before me and they somewhat prejudice my thinking about Him. After all, being a carpenter was not a very prestigious profession.

Jesus was not accepted among the people of His hometown. They marveled at the crowds who gathered to hear the wisdom that came from His mouth. However, they were confused. "Is not this the carpenter?" They thought they knew Jesus too well; they couldn't believe that a simple carpenter could be elevated to the prominence where crowds would gather to hear Him teach.

One man who proclaimed Christ is remembered even today, although he took a vow of poverty and lived a simple life. Saint Francis of Assisi died more than 780 years ago, but he has never been forgotten. Great men and women by the hundreds of thousands have lived and died—kings, conquerors, millionaires, artists, musicians, and scholars. All have been forgotten, but not Saint Francis of Assisi. The world stood back in wonder because he had no money, but he acted as if he were richer than the richest. This little man's body was scarred and wracked with pain, yet he sang sweeter than any bird. He was a beggar who smiled as he dined with the famous and laughed as he shared his last crust with a leper. He learned to love everything that lives as part of God's creation.

> Whoever pursues godliness and unfailing love will find life, righteousness, and honor.
>
> —PROVERBS 21:21 NLT

Saint Francis had a secret worth knowing, and the world has been learning it from him ever since. The secret is the wisdom of Jesus, who some thought was just a carpenter. This plain carpenter was a builder of lives. He used more than lumber to create His structures. He used plain ordinary people just like you and me to further God's kingdom. Isn't that amazing—using common ordinary men and women?

As I am challenged to be like Jesus, may I be like Saint Francis, and not let social status or societal limitations prevent me from becoming the person Christ wants me to become.

> The fear of the Lord is the beginning of knowledge; fools despise wisdom and instruction.
>
> —PROVERBS 1:7

—◊◊◊—

PRAYER: Father God, I, too, can be more than an ordinary carpenter. Light my path so I won't stumble along the way. Amen.

ACTION: Pray about your potential. Ask God how He wants to use you.

REFLECTIONS

Meeting the Fork in the Road

I have set before you life and death, blessings and curses.
Now choose life, so that you and your children may live.
Deuteronomy 30:19

Yogi Berra, the Hall of Fame baseball catcher for the New York Yankees and a renowned humorist, once said, "When you come to a fork in the road, take it." In his typical style, he tells you what to do, but doesn't tell you which fork you must take. You have to figure that out for yourself. Depending upon your point of view of life, you will either go to the right or to the left. If your experience is that of a secularist or that of a man of faith—you might make different choices—one is for life and one is for death. You choose, which one is for you? You can't have your cake and eat it too.

There's something about an illness that makes us think about what's really important in life. It gives us the opportunity to think about the big issues of life. For once, we don't take for granted anything. We also appreciate all the little things we used to take for granted, such as standing up, taking a walk, having a few moments without pain, a child's smile, keeping a good meal down, even a normal bowel movement.

> What a man believes about immortality will color his thinking in every area of life.
>
> —John S. Bonnell

Emilie and I met a fork in the road when our oncologist said, "Emilie, you have cancer!" Our world as we had previously known it came to a screeching halt. Which fork were we going to take—one of hope or one of despair? A good friend of ours shared a very precious verse with us. It is found in John 11:4, which says, "This sickness is not unto death, but for the glory of God, that the Son of God might be glorified thereby" (KJV).

On that day—July 25, 1998—we chose the fork with the higher ground. We claimed this verse as our theme verse during our walk through the valley of the shadow of death. Emilie was going to be healed, and the Lord was going to receive all the glory.

We had to make many choices—some pleasant and some not so pleasant. On some days when Emilie didn't want to make a choice, she would often defer that process to me. She would utter, "Honey, will you choose for me? I just can't." However, there is one choice one can't have someone else make, and that's the choice between life and death. Emilie was the only one who could do that.

There is a choice between life and death—and it's ours to make. When we choose life, we will have victory over death. It's an eternal promise—when we die, we just go from earth to heaven.

> Eternity is not something that begins after you are dead. It is going on all the time. We are in it now.
>
> —CHARLOTTE P. GILMAN

—◈—

PRAYER: Father God, let me have the eternal perspective in life when I come to a fork in the road. Let me choose life over death. Thanks for giving me wisdom to make that good choice. Amen.

ACTION: Go out today and make a heavenly choice.

REFLECTIONS

Say "Yes" for Tomorrow

Rejoice that your names are written in heaven.
LUKE 10:20

We've always been taught that there are no guarantees about tomorrow. Usually that is very true. Scripture tells us that we only have today—enjoy it to the fullest. But there is one way you can say yes for tomorrow.

A few days after Roy Rogers, the western hero of "B" movies, passed away at his home in Apple Valley, California, a local Christian TV station ran a tribute to his life. One of the segments had Dale Evans, Roy's wife, singing a song titled, "Say Yes for Tomorrow." This song was dedicated to the memory of Roy's early decision to put his trust in Jesus as his personal Savior.

> Death is not the enemy of life, but its friend, for it is the knowledge that our years are limited which makes them so precious. It is the truth that time is but lent to us which makes us, at our best, look upon our years as a trust handed into our temporary keeping.
>
> —JOSHUA L. LIEBMAN

While listening to this song, I began to think back over my own life. I said "yes for tomorrow" by saying yes to Jesus when I was 12 years old. My direction for the future was decided at an early age. As I've matured, I've realized many adults have never made this affirmation. What a shame to search all one's life and then, at the end of life, be unsure of what the future might hold.

A very wise man once said, "A wise man does in his youth what a foolish man does in his old age."

If you haven't settled what tomorrow will be, take time today to guarantee your destination. Confirm to your family that you will be united forever in heaven.

> Life without hope is a life without meaning.
> —Unknown

—∿∿—

Prayer: Father God, I thank You for providing a way for me to know where my tomorrows will be. Amen.

Action: If you haven't answered the tomorrow question, today might be the day to settle the most important question in your life.

Reflections

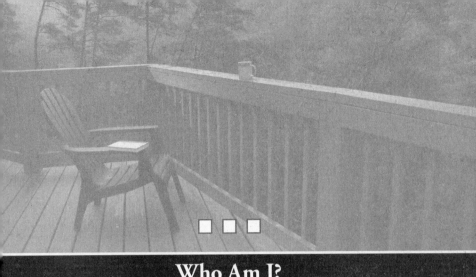

Who Am I?

We are His workmanship, created in Christ Jesus for good works.
EPHESIANS 2:10 NASB

One of the great cries we hear from men is, "Who am I?" We often search for our identity. The Oscar-winning actor Kirk Douglas had a vacation home in Palm Springs, California, and during the winter time, his family would spend the season there. Of course, he was busy and had to return to Beverly Hills during the week, but each Friday afternoon he would drive out to the desert. It was often his custom to pick up a Marine hitchhiking to his base in Yucca Valley. On one occasion, he stopped to pick up one such fellow. The Marine looked into Kirk's Rolls Royce, saw who was driving the car, and let out in a raised voice, "Do you know who you are?"

That so often applies to us! We are a generation of men who don't know who we are. True, our job gives us some indication of our worth, but that's just the tip of the iceberg. A baseball player knows who he is as long as he is playing the sport, but who is he once his playing days are over?

> Tomorrow is the most important thing in life. It comes in to us at midnight very clean. It's perfect when it arrives and puts itself in our hands. It hopes we've learned something from yesterday.
>
> —JOHN WAYNE

Our self-talk may not be too positive but we have to go beyond what whispers we say about ourselves. We even have to cast off what a teacher, a coach, a parent may say who we are. How many of us have heard of the coach who might have told an undersized boy that he will never be good enough to play professional baseball, but here is a young man of 5'10" stature and 160 pounds playing shortstop for a league-leading team?!

No, men, we have to dig deeper to really know who we are. Scripture is full of affirmations of who we are in Christ.

- I am gifted with power, love, and a sound mind (2 Timothy 1:7).
- I am chosen for success (John 15:16).
- I am complete (Colossians 2:9-10).
- I am secure (Romans 8:31-39).
- I am confident (Philippians 1:6).
- I am free (Romans 6:16-18; 8:1-2).
- I am capable (Philippians 4:13).
- I am spiritually alive (Ephesians 2:5).
- I am God's workmanship (Ephesians 2:10).
- I am welcome in God's presence (Ephesians 2:18; Hebrews 4:14-16).
- I am sheltered and protected in God (Colossians 3:3).
- I am valuable to God (1 Corinthians 6:20).
- I am a member of God's family (Ephesians 2:19; 1 John 3:1-2).
- I am God's treasure (1 Peter 2:9-10).
- I am dearly loved (Colossians 3:12).
- I am being transformed (2 Corinthians 3:18).
- I am a new creation (2 Corinthians 5:17).
- I am forgiven (Ephesians 1:6-8).
- I am an heir of God (Romans 8:17).
- I am a friend of God (John 15:15).[6]

Blessed are those who hunger and thirst for righteousness, for they shall be satisfied.

—MATTHEW 5:6 NASB

PRAYER: Father God, give me assurances that I am Your child and that I have all the privileges of being Your child. Amen.

ACTION: Answer this question: "Who am I?"

REFLECTIONS

Cornerstone for Money Management

*Money is an article which may be used as a univer-
sal passport to everywhere except heaven, and as a
universal provider of everything except happiness.*

UNKNOWN

In the building trade, they spend a lot of time determining where and what
will be the cornerstone of a building. In ancient days, we read where the
stonemasons would give a great deal of thought about which stone will be
the cornerstone. They knew that a building would be no stronger than its
cornerstone. The cornerstone determined how the builders would work the
other construction around this valuable anchor for the building.

There are basically four cornerstones for money management.

Cornerstone 1: Recognize that God owns everything. We may possess a lot
of things, but we don't own them. In Haggai 2:8 God states, "The silver is
mine and the gold is mine." Psalm 24:1 properly states, "The earth is the
LORD's, and all it contains, the world, and those who dwell in it" (NASB).
Everything belongs to God. We are merely stewards of His property. God
holds us personally responsible to faithfully manage for Him whatever money
or possessions He allows us to have.

> As caretakers of God's money and property, we must obediently
> grow and nurture the spiritual fruit of self-control.

You might take time to list all of your possessions that God has loaned
you, then take the list and give them to God. This task will consciously
make you realize who really owns all your possessions.

Cornerstone 2: The goal of financial responsibility is financial freedom. In order to be financially free you must meet certain qualifications:

- Your income exceeds your expenses.
- You are able to pay your debts as they fall due.
- You have no unpaid bills.
- Above all, you are content at your present income level.

If you are not satisfied with what you have, you will never be satisfied with what you want.

Cornerstone 3: Establish a spiritual purpose for your life. If your spiritual purpose is to serve God (Matthew 6:33), all of your resources become ministering currency toward that end. The more money we give to God's work, the more our hearts will be fixed on Him. The opposite is also true. Don't give money to God's work, and your heart will not be fixed on Him.

All couples daily have to prioritize how they will spend their money. How you choose to spend your money is determined by what you think about God. If you vote for God, you will readily be sensitive to those things that have eternal value. If you lean toward the world view you will shy away from godly venture, but your spending will be more terminal than eternal. Look at your last six months of expenditures from your credit card statements and your checkbook entries and you will soon see where your values are—earthly or heavenly.

Cornerstone 4: Give money to the Lord on a regular basis. For the Christian, the only reason to be rich is to have resources to carry on God's program. Does God need our wealth? No! Can God's purposes be carried out without our money? Yes! God doesn't need our possessions, but we do need to give. It's good for the soul.

God doesn't care how much we give as deeply as He cares why we give. When we lovingly and obediently fulfill our role as givers—no matter what the amount—God will use what we give to minister to others, and we will receive a blessing in return. The Scriptures clearly show us many directions for our giving:

- To God through our tithes, gifts, and offerings (Proverbs 3:9-10; 1 Corinthians 16:2).
- To the poor (Proverbs 19:17).
- To other believers in need (Romans 12:13; Galatians 6:9-10).

- To those who minister to us (Galatians 6:6; 1 Timothy 5:17-18).
- To widows (1 Timothy 5:3-16).
- To family members (1 Timothy 5:8).

Christians are clearly instructed to return to the Owner of everything a portion of what He has given us. With that in mind, here are some common financial mistakes:

- Attempting to get rich too fast.
- Believing the credit-card delusion.
- Not taking advantage of your benefit plans at work.
- Overpaying your home mortgage. Lower your cost by refinancing.
- Paying too much for all of your insurance policies.
- Investing for your children's college education the wrong way.
- Falling for a "hot tip."

―∾―

PRAYER: Father God, let these four cornerstones be what I will build my financial planning on. I want to be a good steward of the money you have given me. Amen.

ACTION: Take one of these cornerstones each week for four weeks and improve your money management.

Because the Lord is my Shepherd,
I have everything I need!
He lets me rest in the meadow grass
and leads me beside the quiet streams.
He gives me new health.
He helps me do what honors him the most.
Even when walking through the dark valley of death
I will not be afraid, for you are close beside me,
guarding, guiding all the way.

You provide delicious food for me
in the presence of my enemies.
You have welcomed me as your guest;
blessings overflow!
Your goodness and unfailing kindness shall
be with me all of my life,
and afterwards I will live with you
forever in your home.

—PSALM 23 TLB

REFLECTIONS

Often the Truth Hurts

It is better, if it is God's will, to suffer for
doing good than for doing evil.
1 PETER 3:15

We live in a world which teaches us to be popular. We want everyone to like us. Who wants to be unpopular? As you look around your community you can identify the in-group. They drive the most popular car, live in the most popular neighborhood, go to the most popular restaurant, visit the most popular resorts, and wear the most popular sunglasses.

To be popular, you have to fit the mold that establishes what is popular. To step out from the crowd and be unpopular is seldom found, and to do that is never popular with the masses.

However, in 1517, Martin Luther nailed his Ninety-five Theses to the door of the castle church in Wittenberg. Luther became known as a reformer, and we remember his bold stand as a turning point in church history.

This priest exhibited great character of courage at criticizing the church's practice of selling forgiveness through indulgences, which ultimately could lead people to think that whenever they sinned, they could just purchase forgiveness, thus making them less inclined to avoid sin.

Luther's passion and zeal to prevent these practices did not make him popular with the Catholic leaders of his day. In fact, he became very unpopular.

There are times in each of our lives we must make a stand to speak words that are unpopular. As dads, we will have to say no, a word which is not always well-received by our children. As a businessman, you will have to say no when a business associate wants you to bend the rules to accommodate a client. As an actor, you might have to say no to a movie script that portrays sin that is not comfortable for you. Yes, there will be times in all our lives when we have to say no.

Living for God is about doing the right thing, even when it's unpopular.

> Right is right no matter how few are doing it and wrong is wrong no matter how many are doing it.
>
> —Unknown

Having God's Word in our hearts doesn't always result in warm, pleasant feelings. Sometimes God's Word starts a blazing forest fire in one's soul, causing us to challenge mainstream America. You might be called on to stand and call a spade a spade.

> Unclean in the sight of God is everyone who is unrighteous: clean therefore is everyone who is righteous; if not in the sight of men yet in the sight of God, who judges without error.
>
> —St. Augustine

―ᴧᴧᴧ―

PRAYER: Father God, let me be brave when I need to be. I want to have the courage to be unpopular when I have to stand for Your righteousness. Amen.

ACTION: Be willing to make a stand today when it might make you unpopular.

REFLECTIONS

Why Pray?

Hallowed be thy name.
MATTHEW 6:9 KJV

We often ask ourselves, why pray? God knows the beginning from the end, He has appointed every day of our lives, then why pray? During my lifetime, I've asked the same question. I've had doubt and dry periods in my walk with God. You could make a graph of these varying points and they would look like your favorite stock market graph. There would be highs, lows, and even plateaus.

During Emilie's illness, I felt the closest to God. He became so real to me. My prayers were more than, "Now I lay me down to sleep. I pray the Lord my soul to keep. God bless Mommy, Daddy, brother, and sister." I went from drinking milk to eating grown-up food. I finally knew what it meant to have a strong relationship with God. I gained two important insights on prayer:

1. If God is willing to give me the greatest imaginable gift of all—Himself—then what good thing would He ever withhold from me?

   If God is for us, who is against us? He who did not spare His own Son, but delivered Him up for us all, how will He not also with Him freely give us all things?

   —ROMANS 8:31-32 NASB

2. Whether I realize it or not, all that I ever ask for in prayer

is in the final analysis and at the deepest level, a desire or need for the activity of the Holy Spirit to be more real and effective in my life.

> My grace is sufficient for you, for power is perfected in weakness. Most gladly, therefore, I will rather boast about my weaknesses, that the power of Christ may dwell in me…for when I am weak, then I am strong.
>
> —2 Corinthians 12:9-10 nasb

I began to understand that all things come from God. I receive the good and the bad of life because I know that He is the potter, and I'm the clay. He can make and mold me in His own way. I've learned to turn over the events of life to His will for my life. Through life's experiences, I've been able to say, "Thy will be done in my life."

Therefore, when I pray, I close my prayer, like Charles Spurgeon, by saying to God, "If there is anything I have prayed for that would not be good for me, please do not grant it." God is good—all the time.

Why pray? I must pray in order to understand who God is and what an amazing experience it is to be in His presence. I must have someone greater than me in order to get through this maze of life.

The Lord's Prayer

Our Father which
art in heaven,
Hallowed be thy name.
Thy kingdom come.
Thy will be done in earth,
as it is in heaven.
Give us this day our
daily bread.
And forgive us our debts
as we forgive our debtors.
And lead us not into
temptation, but deliver us
from evil:
For thine is the kingdom,
and the power, and the
glory, for ever. Amen.

Matthew 6:9-13 kjv

PRAYER: Father God, never let me lose the desire to be in Your presence each day of my life. I need that two-way conversation. Amen.

ACTION: If you aren't in the habit I ask you to pray for 21 consecutive days. Just you and God.

REFLECTIONS

Check Your Joy Meter

*I have told you this so that my joy may be in
you and that your joy may be complete.*
John 15:11

Several years ago when I was a vice president, general manager of a midsize modular home manufacturer, we took 200 of our top distributors on a vacation trip to Jamaica. This trip has given us many wonderful memories over the years. With us on the trip were many of our dealers and corporate executives and their wives.

As our plane landed on this small island, all the passengers departed the stair ramp with mixed emotions. Some expressed pure delight in the warmth of the weather, the beauty of the water, and the fresh smells of cut fruit and vegetables. Delight was even expressed about our mode of transportation to the hotel and its lovely tropical landscaped facilities.

> There are no secrets to success. It is the result of preparation, hard work, and learning from failure.
>
> —Colin L. Powell

However, as is to be expected in any cross-section of people, some expressed their disdain for all the same features that most of us were joyful about. Our mouths hung open in disbelief at the complaints of some disgruntled vacationers in such a romantic and gorgeous setting, topped off by the most ideal climate you would ever want to experience.

The next morning as we approached the elevators to take us to the main lobby for breakfast, we were met by the most delightful group of young Jamaican housekeepers. They were singing, laughing, and thanking God for such a beautiful new day. All of a sudden, Emilie and I were made aware of the contrast between the various groups at the hotel.

Many of the wealthiest members of our group were moaning in negative tones, yet these low-income young ladies were expressing sheer joy for their abundance. Later we were to find out that these housekeepers went to mission schools and had been grounded in the fundamentals of the Christian faith.

The young girls certainly reflected the joy of Jesus in their behavior and their testimony to the people around them. They weren't joyful because of status, wealth, or possessions, but because Jesus told them they could have joy. It's that simple: Each day we can choose to be full of joy. We can respond to other people any way we want, but Scripture says that we can have the joy of Christ in our lives, and that it can be complete.

This means it doesn't take any more than Jesus (no wealth, no status, no possessions, but just Jesus) to make our joy complete. No longer can we say that we would have joy if only we had _____.

> Real joy comes not from ease or riches, or from the praise of men, but from doing something worthwhile.
>
> —WILFRED T. GRENFELL

PRAYER: Father God, I truly want to reflect in my life the joy that You have given me. Life would be just a gloomy day without Your influence upon my life. Amen.

ACTION: Ask this question around the dinner table tonight, "How do people show that they have joy in their lives?"

REFLECTIONS

Understanding Your Finances

You may say to yourself, "My power and the strength of my hands have produced this wealth for me." But remember the LORD your God, for it is he who gives you the ability to produce wealth.
DEUTERONOMY 8:17-18

For the Christian family, good money management is imperative for at least three reasons.

First, God associates our ability to handle money with our spirituality. In Luke 16:11, Jesus states, "If you have not been trustworthy in handling worldly wealth, who will trust you with true riches?" If we want to grow in spiritual responsibility and blessing, we must prove our faithfulness in the area of financial responsibility. God is not going to trust us spiritually if we have been irresponsible with our money.

Second, financial responsibility is important because we are only caretakers of what really belongs to God. Psalm 24:1 declares, "The earth is the LORD's, and all it contains" (NASB).

You may possess many things—home, car, furniture, boat, money, but you don't own anything. Even your ability to earn more comes from God. Everything belongs to Him; we are merely stewards of His property (see Deuteronomy 8:17-18). God holds us personally responsible to faithfully manage for Him whatever money or possessions He allows us to have.

> The wise man saves for the future, but the foolish man spends whatever he gets.
>
> —PROVERBS 21:20 TLB

Often we are tempted to grasp our possessions selfishly as if they belong to us and not to God.

As caretakers of God's money and property we must obediently grow and nurture the spiritual fruit of self-control (see Galatians 5:22-23). Every couple we have counseled over the years regarding money problems have had at least one member who lacked self-control. Money problems were just one of many undisciplined areas in their lives, including maintenance of the home, yard, automobile, spiritual life, personal hygiene, children, and on and on. These couples exemplify the "easy come, easy go" generation. They are irresponsible with their money and possessions and consequently always have problems in these areas. God wants to give to us abundantly, but He also wants us to exercise self-control over the management of what He gives.

Third, financial responsibility is necessary to help us avoid a number of major money mistakes. Most couples fall into one or more of the following traps because they have not appropriated biblically based principles for the use of their money and possessions.

1. *Getting into debt beyond our means to repay.* Easily available credit can become a problem when we have no predetermined limits and guidelines for spending.

2. *Living a money-centered life.* Scripture warns us that God is to be our focus, not money (see Matthew 6:19-24 and 1 Timothy 6:6-10).

3. *Trying to get rich quick.* Don't be lured into get-rich schemes. If it sounds too good to be true, it probably is. Proper money management will help you keep tantalizing schemes in perspective (see Proverbs 28:22).

4. *Withholding benevolence.* Proverbs 11:24-25 teaches us that if we give generously to God and others, we will receive everything we need. As Christians we are to be givers and not grabbers.

5. *Using people.* Don't use people as stepping stones to promotions or personal gain, or see people as merely customers. Instead we are to love, honor, and care for our friends.

6. *Misplacing priorities.* When we overemphasize money in our lives, we try to beat God's system and do things our

own way. The order of the big three priorities in life—God, family, and work—often get wrongly aligned as either "work, family, and God"; "work, God, and family"; "family, work, and God"; or "family, God, and work."

It is more blessed to give than to receive.

—ACTS 20:35

We all have to ask ourselves this basic question: "How much of my soul am I going to sell to my boss?" Until we stand up and say, "No more," will you be satisfied with your proper listing of your priorities. Let them be this way: "God, family, and work."

> Show me the way
> Not to fortune and fame,
> not how to win laurels
> or praise for my name—
> But show me the way
> To spread "the Great Story"
> That Thine is the Kingdom
> and Power and Glory.

—HELEN STEINER RICE

———

PRAYER: Father God, I realize that money management is one of the great areas of responsibility for me as a husband. May I apply these principles to my life. Amen.

ACTION: Evaluate what needs to be improved in this money area. Start today to make critical changes.

REFLECTIONS

Live for Today

*May the God of hope fill you with all the joy and peace as
you trust in him, so that you may overflow with hope...*
ROMANS 15:13

Yesterday is gone, tomorrow is in the present, and today is all we have. In fact, we have no assurance that we will even be here to experience tomorrow.

As I've observed my five grandchildren over the years, one thing stands out very vividly—their ability to live and enjoy the moment. They can take the "now" and make it a gift. I'm trying to forget about what happened yesterday and stop thinking about what might happen tomorrow. I just want to experience the fullness of today.

In order to capture the present, we need to give less attention to worries, mistakes, what's going wrong, general concerns, things to get done, the past, the future, and the undone.

> Saint Francis of Assisi was hoeing his garden when someone asked what he would do if he were suddenly to learn that he would die before sunset that very day. "I would finish hoeing my garden," he replied.
>
> —LOUIS FISCHER

Today I will only think about today. No regrets for the past or fears about the future. When you do this, all your focus is on the now. You can smile, laugh, pray, think, and enjoy what each moment brings.

Often our anxieties are about situations we have no control over. One of the Barnes' mottos is, "Eighty-five percent of the things we worry about never happen." Why spend all that negative energy on something that probably will never happen?

We are to stop and smell the roses, hear the train whistle, see the puffy clouds in the sky, enjoy the rainfall, and watch the snow flurries. When we begin to see and experience every minute of the present, we will also begin to see the grandeur of God and His vastness.

> I shall not pass this way again;
> Then let me now relieve some pain,
> Remove some barrier from the road,
> Or brighten someone's heavy load.
>
> —EVA ROSE YORK

PRAYER: Father God, let me learn to live for the "now." I truly want to observe all that You have given to me. Amen.

ACTION: Cancel all your business appointments for the afternoon. Call your wife, and do something you normally wouldn't do.

REFLECTIONS

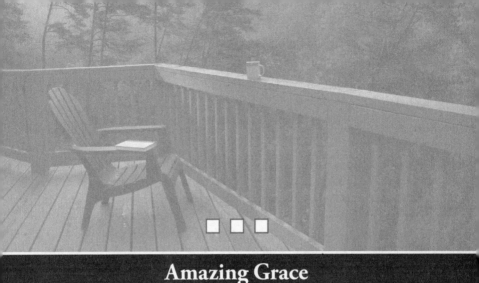

Amazing Grace

By grace you have been saved through faith.

EPHESIANS 2:8 NASB

While celebrating a recent wedding anniversary, Emilie and I had the good fortune to cruise the Mexican waters on the "Love Boat." It was truly a wonderful experience. We visited the main Pacific Ocean seaports, had great weather, enjoyed outstanding food, and met several new friends. One of the highlights of our trip happened one Sunday evening as we were leaving the harbor of Acapulco. Bagpipers started playing the Christian anthem "Amazing Grace." That five-minute concert was such a spiritual uplift that we have never forgotten it. It certainly added a positive insight to our salvation when we paused on the top deck of that large cruise ship and reflected that it is only by God's grace that we are saved.

In a small cemetery in a parish churchyard in Olney, England, stands a granite tombstone with the following inscription:

> John Newton, Clerk, once an infidel and libertine, a servant of slavers in Africa, was by the rich mercy of our Lord and Savior Jesus Christ, preserved, restored, pardoned, and appointed to preach the faith he had long labored to destroy.[7]

John Newton never ceased to marvel at the grace of God that had so dramatically transformed him from his early life as an African slave trader to a proclaimer of the glorious gospel of Christ. This was always the dominant theme of his preaching and writing. In 1779, Newton wrote these words:

Amazing grace! how sweet the sound!
That saved a wretch like me!
I once was lost, but now am found;
Was blind, but now I see.

Even though we aren't slave traders, our sins are just as great. Without the grace of God we would all remain sinners doomed to eternal death, but with God's grace we can live eternally in heaven with Him and His saints. We are saved through Jesus, not of ourselves and not of any of our words. Salvation is a gift from God. Truly it is amazing grace.

—⁓—

PRAYER: Father God, thank You for Your free gift of grace. May we always appreciate Your love for us. Amen.

ACTION: Give praises to God today for your salvation.

REFLECTIONS

Watch Your Self-talk

*How precious it is, Lord, to realize that you are think-
ing about me constantly! I can't even count how
many times a day your thoughts turn to me.*
PSALM 139:17 TLB

If God is thinking good thoughts about me, why shouldn't I think good thoughts about myself? God says that I'm more important than the birds of the air. He made me in His image, yet I speak to myself thoughts that don't sound like I believe that I am His child.

What we think in our minds makes a great impact on who we believe we are. Do you ever catch your thoughts taking a negative turn? As you check your self-talk, do you realize that a lot of junk is crossing your mind? Most of us are very good at criticizing ourselves. We find fault with ourselves very easily.

> If you doubt you can accomplish something, then you can't accomplish it. You have to have confidence in your ability, and then be tough enough to follow through.
>
> —ROSALYNN CARTER

I suggest that you develop a more positive thought process. When I know that God is thinking about me constantly, how can I not think positively about myself? If I am worthy to Him, why should I not be worthy to myself? As you look in the mirror of life, you shouldn't be afraid to say out loud and clear, "Good job." We aren't being conceited when we recognize the good in life—however, we must recognize that all good comes from our heavenly Father.

After each breakthrough in life, give yourself a celebration. It's okay to say, "You've done a good job." Keep telling yourself the positive—don't let the negative take hold of your thought process.

> Let no unwholesome word proceed from your mouth, but only such a word as is good for edification according to the need of the moment...
>
> —EPHESIANS 4:29 NASB

PRAYER: Father God, knowing that You are thinking about me has often given me extra strength to carry on for another day. Your thoughts are precious to me! Amen.

ACTION: Look in your mirror and say with confidence, "Good job."

REFLECTIONS

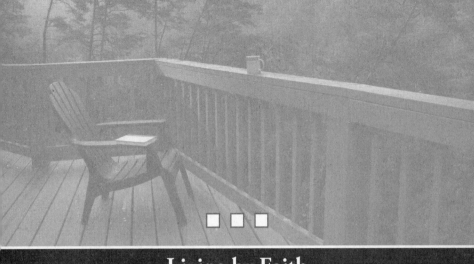

Living by Faith

*Now faith is the assurance of things hoped
for, the conviction of things not seen.*
HEBREWS 11:1 NASB

I often hear people say, "Have enough faith," or "I have faith that this or that will happen." What do we really mean by the word *faith*? In Hebrews 11:1, we read that it is the assurance (meaning you have no doubt at all) of things hoped for (much more than hoped for), the conviction of things not seen.

> Faith is the confidence that God is who He says He is and will
> do everything He has promised to do.
>
> —ANDY STANLEY

The Christian has two choices on how he looks upon faith:

- circumstantial faith
- Christian faith

Circumstantial faith. We're not sure that there is a God. Some people believe in Him, but when I've prayed in the past, I don't seem to get my answer as I've prayed. If I do get it, it's delayed and not as soon as I would have liked. When the challenge of life shows its ugly head, I pray as the last hurdle. I try to solve the pressure by my own power, by my cleverness—when this fails then I might reach out to God for some help.

I often wait until I or my family gets sick, has an accident, or is on the verge of death—maybe God can heal, but only after I've tried all my connections.

Oh, I thought the new home, the new luxury automobile, that next vacation at a five-star resort would give me the pleasures that I've been looking for, but they only seem to pull me farther from knowing God in a personal way.

Yes, I have strong faith when all's going well and I have no emergencies in my life. I guess my faith is a "fair-weather faith." If it's convenient I will believe in it, but if God doesn't respond to my every beck and call, He may not be my God. God is good, but not all the time.

Christian faith. The Christian who knows that "God is good—all the time" is one who keeps his eyes on Jesus, who initiates and perfects our faith. Our knowledge of God does not depend on our circumstances. No matter what our experiences are in life—the ups and the downs—our faith should be that God is able to do all He says in Scripture. If He says it (in Scripture), that settles it.

> Fixing our eyes on Jesus, the author and perfecter of faith, who for the joy set before Him endured the cross, despising the shame, and has set down at the right hand of the throne of God.
>
> —HEBREWS 12:2 NASB

He is the Alpha and the Omega. He knows the beginning from the end. He is the potter, and we are the clay. He knew me before I was born.

Faith is not some unknown force or power or Karma that will get us through our situation. Faith is knowing who our object of faith is—Jesus.

Yes, even in times of illness, death, divorce, the change in our economy, or a failed business, we can trust and depend on God. He will never depart or forsake us in our time of need.

In Job 2:9-10, we read the conversation between Job and his wife. She asks him a question regarding the tragic events in their family's life: "Do you still hold fast your integrity? Curse God and die."

Job replied as a man of true faith: "Shall we indeed accept good from God and not accept adversity?" (NASB).

By Job's reply, we know that he has a godly faith—one that goes beyond the circumstances of life. In essence, Job shouted out with a clear and powerful voice, "God is good—all the time."

Which faith do you live by—the faith depending on circumstances, or the Christian faith that stays faithful in spite of the circumstances?

—∽∿∾—

Prayer: Father God, I truly want Job's faith. I want to stand on the promises that God has given us in His Word. Give me the courage and strength to be faithful in all of life's valleys. Amen.

Action: In your daily readings of Scripture begin to identify the many promises that have been given to us as believers.

Reflections

He Cares for Me

Let him have all your worries and cares, for he is always think-
ing about you and watching everything that concerns you.
1 PETER 5:7 TLB

Have you ever asked yourself how God can know you? I ask, "How can God know little old me? There are SO many people to take care of." But soon I realize that if He cares for the birds of the air, knows the number of hairs on my head, and can count all the number of sand pebbles on the beach, He can certainly care for me.

I'm from the old generation that sang hymns full of theology, and it's hard for me to get used to singing the new worship songs. Some of these great old hymns are "It Is Well with My Soul" and "A Mighty Fortress Is Our God." We are not big or strong enough to carry all our worries by ourselves. We need help, and Jesus is there to lighten our load. Without Him, I would have been crushed under the load—it was too heavy.

—◦◦◦—

PRAYER: Father God, thank You that Your Spirit knows how to pray for me, even when I do not. I rely on Your Holy Spirit to make the depth of my heart known to You this very day. Amen.

He has not promised we will never feel lonely,
But He has promised that in Him
We will never be alone.

He has not promised that we will be free
From pain and sorrow,
But He has promised He will be our help,
Our strength, our everlasting peace.

No matter what happens in our lives,
We can believe fully in His promise…
We can rest confidently in His love.

—AUTHOR UNKNOWN

REFLECTIONS

Just Keep on Pedaling

Trust in the LORD with all your heart and lean not
on your own understanding; in all your ways acknowl-
edge him, and he will make your paths straight.
PROVERBS 3:5-6

At first I saw God as my observer, my judge, keeping a list of the things I did wrong, so as to know whether I merited heaven or hell when I die. He was out there sort of like the President. I knew He was out there, but I didn't really know Him.

But later on when I recognized God, it seemed as though life was rather like a bike ride, but it was a tandem bike, and I noticed that God was in the back helping me pedal.

I don't know just when it was that He suggested we change places, but life has not been the same since. Life without my God, that is. God makes life exciting!

When I had control, I knew the way. It was rather boring, but predictable. It was the shortest distance between two points. But when He took the lead, He knew delightful long cuts, up mountains, through rocky places, and at breakneck speeds! It was all I could do to hang on! Even though it looked like madness, He said, "Pedal!"

I worried and was anxious and asked, "Where are you taking me?" He laughed and didn't answer. I started to learn to trust. I forgot my boring life and entered into the adventure. And when I'd say "I'm scared," He'd lean back and touch my hand.

He took me to people with gifts that I needed—the gifts of healing, acceptance, and joy. They gave me their gifts to take on my journey—our journey, God's and mine. And we were off again. He said, "Give the gifts away. They're extra baggage, too much weight." So I did, to the people we met, and I found that in giving I received, and still our burden was light.

I did not trust Him in control of my life at first. I thought He'd wreck it. But He knows bike secrets. He knows how to make it bend to take sharp corners, jump to clear high rocks, fly to shorten scary passages.

And I am learning to shut up and pedal in the strangest places, and I'm beginning to enjoy the view and the cool breeze on my face with my delightful companion, my God.

And when I'm sure I just can't do any more, He smiles and says, "Pedal."[8]

When some people say, "Oh, life is so boring I don't even want to get up in the morning," we can't comprehend that kind of mind-set. We find life so exciting that our feet bound out of bed each day anticipating what God has in store for us.

Each day is a real adventure. Many days God just says, "Come along and trust me." It would be nice to know every detail, what lies beyond each ridge and what's around each of the corners of life, but God very patiently says, "Just trust me. You do the pedaling and I'll do the leading." Our reply is often, "Are you sure You know the way? What if You make a mistake with my life? But God, I've never been this way before. What if…" The dialogue can go on for hours, days, and months, but eventually we arrive to the point where we say, "God, You lead, and I'll keep on pedaling."

As our key verse says today, we are to trust in the Lord with all our heart and lean not on our own understanding. That's so hard to do if we're not used to turning over our lives to Someone who is bigger than us. Just relax and let God be all that He says He is—trustworthy.[9]

—◦◦◦—

PRAYER: Father God, let me slow down so I can trust You to direct my paths. God, You lead and I'll keep on pedaling.

ACTION: List in your journal four things that have been bother-
ing you, and that you want to give to God.

REFLECTIONS

Better Than Your Money Market

May he multiply you a thousand times
more and bless you as promised.
DEUTERONOMY 1:11 TLB

A wise couple will establish a plan to save part of their wages for the rainy day. One basic lesson in finances is to spend less than you make. There needs to be a definite goal to set up a savings plan when you are young, then when you are old you will have a good retirement account for those golden years. Don't wait until you are into mid-life. That's too late! Start wherever you find yourself.

Today's Scripture tells me that God will multiply my efforts by one thousand percent, plus He will also bless you. God loves trustworthy and faithful stewards. If you are faithful in a little, He will give you more and more blessings. In today's financial market one is lucky to get a conservative 2-3 percent interest on one's investments. But a 1000 percent markup is simply unbelievable. Yet this is exactly what I am promised in Scripture. The Lord has promised to increase my blessings too.

Of course, this verse is talking about more than money or possessions. It's also talking about a return on investment in family, emotional stability, marriage, health, desires, goals, and all other components of life. And it doesn't have a time limit, either. Perhaps some of the blessings I'm promised will happen in eternity and in the lives of those who come after me on this earth.

Know that God keeps His promises—and what a promise this is.

Knowing that my blessings are growing and growing and growing gives me strength—even amid the uncertainties of life.

Always allow honesty and integrity to increase with your riches.

—Unknown

—⁓⁓—

PRAYER: Father God, sometimes I am discouraged by the "daili-ness" of life. Calm me today. Help me to set my sights on things that have eternal value. Amen.

ACTION: May I be a blessing to someone today!

REFLECTIONS

Your Big Mess Is a Blessing

If anyone does not provide for his relatives, and espe-
cially for his immediate family, he has denied
the faith and is worse than an unbeliever.

1 TIMOTHY 5:8

Billy, would you please help with the dishes tonight? I've had such a long hard day at work, and I just don't have the energy to do one more thing." Billy's reply is like that of many teenagers: "But Dad, I wasn't the only one to make the mess. The rest of the family needs to help out too. I just hate dirty dishes. Why can't we use paper plates?"

Does this conversation sound familiar to you? Who likes the mess that goes with the meal? Wouldn't it be great if somehow the dishes took care of themselves? But of course, they don't; messes do need attention.

> You will find as you look back upon your life, that the moments
> that stand out are the moments when you have done things
> for others.
>
> —HENRY DRUMMOND

Much of life is how we look at things. Are you positive or negative? Is your glass half-full or half-empty?

Let's see if we can turn the messes of our life into blessings. In order for us to have dirty dishes, it means that we have food, and in most cases more food than we need. We have leftovers, which means we have an abundance of food rather than the mess it makes. In America most of us are truly blessed to have enough food on our table.

Let us as dads teach our family members to thank God for the messes in life. How many of our messes are simply evidence that God has given us abundance? Let's look at our messes in a new light: How are they signs of abundance?

- How about clothes that need washing and ironing?
- Lawns that need to be mowed?
- Beds that need to be made?
- Carpets that need vacuuming?
- A refrigerator that needs cleaning?
- A school that we need to walk to?
- A job that we need to drive to?
- A home that needs painting?
- A television that needs repairs?

Build for your team a feeling of oneness, of depending on one another and of strength to be derived by unity.

—VINCE LOMBARDI

PRAYER: Father God, thank You for showing me that I need to be reminded that our messes are really a sign of abundance and that You are the One who so richly gives to us. Amen.

ACTION: As a family, discuss the messes of your lives. How are they really indications that God has given us an abundance?

REFLECTIONS

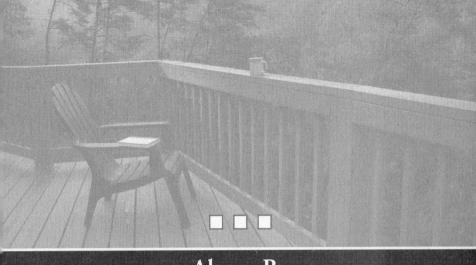

Always Be

Always be joyful. Always keep on praying. No matter
what happens, always be thankful, for this is God's
will for you who belong to Christ Jesus.
1 Thessalonians 5:16-18 tlb

Two good commands: 1) Always be joyful. 2) Always be thankful. If we could master these two ideas, we would have it made in life. We men need to reflect these two traits to our wives and to our children. From them we can branch out to our neighbors and people at work. I find that a lot of men have difficulty being joyful and thankful. We have to learn to live a more fun-filled life. Men often take life too seriously.

If the Bible says it, I want to believe it. That's a good slogan to live by—as long as we go beyond just believing with our minds and begin to obey with our lives. The Bible means what it says, and that's important to keep in mind.

Today's Scripture tells us always be joyful, always keep praying, always be thankful. Even when we try it is seldom always. That's tough to "always be"—but when God says "always" He means always. For God's men, joy, prayer, and thanksgiving are to be constants.

Real joy comes not from ease or riches or from the praise of men,
but from doing something worthwhile.

—Wilfred T. Grenfell

We are to stay simple and pure before the Lord, living out these three attributes of the Christian life consistently. When we do, we not only live in the full flow of God's blessings, but we reflect those blessings to the world around us. Remember, you might be the only Bible some will ever read.

We can't do it without God's help, of course. But that's the heart of the Good News. He's always with us.

> In ordinary life we hardly realize that we receive a great deal more than we give, and that it is only with gratitude that life becomes rich. It is very easy to overestimate the importance of our own achievements in comparison with what we owe others.
>
> —Dietrich Bonhoeffer

PRAYER: Father God, flowers, colors, textures, rain, sunshine, water, soil; You are the Creator of them all. Produce Your love and goodness in me! Amen.

ACTION: Make joy, prayer, and thanksgiving a part of your daily walk.

REFLECTIONS

Make Today Forgiveness Day

Forgive us our debts, as we also have forgiven our debtors.
MATTHEW 6:12 NASB

In our hearts we sometimes store unforgiven words to God, to ourselves, to a family member, to a neighbor, or to someone at work. When we have not forgiven, we become captive to that act and it holds us prisoner until we forgive. So we need to clean that slate of unforgiveness to release and let go.

Forgiveness is very costly; there can be pain when we seek to forgive. Yet Jesus forgave while on the cross, and we have to do it as well. True forgiveness from us to others isn't possible unless we have experienced God's forgiveness to us. We can't give away what we haven't experienced ourselves.

We first have to let God forgive us before we can forgive others. Out of our gratitude for God's forgiveness to us, we are able to understand this whole area of forgiveness. When we are right with God, we want to get right with others.

The only person who is a slave to unforgiveness is the one who is harboring it toward someone else. When we consider this area of forgiveness, we think of three groups of people:

- Those who need forgiveness.
- Those with whom we need to seek forgiveness.
- Those who need our help in forgiving others.

Our longest list would be found in group two above. In Scripture, Jesus says that we are to be forgiven of our sins as we forgive those who sin against us. We cannot be forgiven unless we forgive. Unconfessed forgiveness clogs up our spiritual arteries. We will never have good blood flow to our hearts until we get rid of what clogs us up. God wants to go to our hearts, but we can't receive His blessings and abundance because we need to clean up this matter called "unforgiveness."

One of God's biblical principles is that unforgiving people cannot receive forgiveness. Jesus didn't say that it wouldn't be painful. Many times it is. However, to become fresh in our Christian walk, we must clean the slate of all the marks we have logged against others. Then God can flow freely in our lives.

> If we confess our sins, he is faithful and just and will forgive us our sins and purify us from all unrighteousness.
>
> —1 John 1:9

Prayer: Father God, let me jump to forgive today. Let today become forgiveness day. Would You please go ahead of me and make the hearts before me tender and prepare them for my request? Amen.

Action: Make today "Forgiveness Day."

Reflections

Ten Rules That Work

Remember the Sabbath day by keeping it holy.
Exodus 20:8

In looking at great success, we find certain strands that weave through a family, a career, a marriage, a church, or any kind of organization that rises above the commonness we see in everyday life. Sam Walton of Wal-Mart is a household name. His is one of the most recognizable names in the history of American business.

In Sam's autobiography, he gives ten principles that worked for his business. As we look at these, we can transfer the concepts to our marriage and/or business.

1. *Commit to your business.* Believe in it more than anyone else. Create a passion for it.

2. *Share your profits.* Treat all members of the company as partners. Behave as a servant leader in the partnership.

3. *Motivate your partners.* Each day think of new and more interesting ways to motivate and challenge your partners.

4. *Communicate everything you possibly can to your partners.* The more they know, the more they will understand.

5. *Appreciate everything your associates do for the business.* Nothing else can quite substitute for a few well-chosen, well-timed sincere words of praise.

6. *Celebrate your successes.* Don't take yourself too seriously, loosen up, have fun, laugh often, and show enthusiasm often.

7. *Listen to everyone in your company.* Figure out ways to get the partners talking. Listen when they do talk.

8. *Exceed your customer's expectations.* Stand behind everything you do. Customers will come back when they are valued.

9. *Control your expenses better than your competition.* You can make a lot of different mistakes and still recover if you run an efficient operation.

10. *Swim upstream.* Go the other way. Ignore the conventional wisdom. You can find your niche by going in exactly the opposite direction.[10]

As God gave Moses the Ten Commandments, which have guided civilized man throughout history, He has also given good business people basic principles which help structure the workings of a successful marriage and/or business. All of these principles are useful in establishing basic guidelines for our lives as Christians—develop a plan and begin to purposely live out that plan. Don't drift through life looking for direction; it can easily be found. You have to take hold of it and make it part of your life.

> An ideal marriage is one in which two people love, cherish, and encourage each other through all the troubles caused by their marriage.
>
> —Unknown

PRAYER: Father God, let me take both sets of today's principles (marriage and business) and make them part of my life. Help me integrate both sets into my everyday life. Amen.

ACTION: Review the ten principles by Sam Walton and see how they can apply to a successful marriage and family life.

REFLECTIONS

The Rewards of Friendship

He who has found his life will lose it, and he who
has lost his life for my sake will find it.
MATTHEW 10:39 NASB

You probably don't need to be convinced, but friendship does indeed offer rich rewards. Consider the comments of these people:

- Upon the death of his friend A.H. Hallam, the poet Tennyson declared, "Tis better to have loved and lost than never to have loved at all."

- Helen Keller once said, "With the death of every friend I have loved a part of me has been buried, but their contribution to my being of happiness, strength and understanding remains to sustain me in an altered world."

- Jesus taught that we find ourselves when we lose ourselves (Matthew 10:39).

When have you experienced these truths about friendship? The value of friendship extends beyond emotional closeness and connectedness. Research, for instance, shows that lonely people live significantly shorter lives than the general public.

What do you think of when you think of friendship? Intimate sharing? Talking about feelings and hurts and hopes?

The fact seems to stand that women have an easier time with friendships than men do. Our culture, for instance, permits women to be closer to each other than men can be with one another. Women can hug, cry, hold hands, and interlock their arms as they walk down the street, but men are not as free to do these things.

> It is the steady and merciless increase of occupations, the augmented speed at which we are always trying to live, the crowding of each day with more work than it can profitably hold, which has cost us, among other things, the undisturbed enjoyment of friends. Friendship takes time, and we have no time to give it.

> —AGNES REPPLIER

Friendships are another difference between men and women, especially in marriage. Men are activity-oriented, and women are relationally-oriented. If you're married, simply get interested in your wife's activities. That's one way you can be her friend. After all, "You have to be a friend in order to have a friend."

—⁓—

PRAYER: Father God, I realize that there is a difference on how men and women look at friendship so differently. May I have the proper discernment to make my wife my friend. Amen.

ACTION: Take your wife on a date and watch one of her favorite kinds of movie. Get an ice-cream cone after the movie.

REFLECTIONS

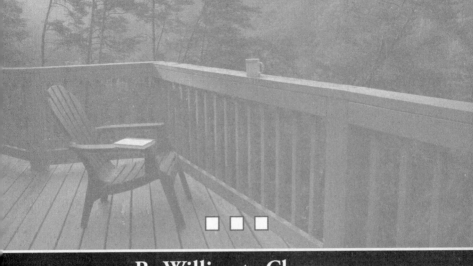

Be Willing to Change

Do not be conformed to this world, but be transformed by
the renewing of your mind, that you may prove what the will
of God is, that which is good and acceptable and perfect.
ROMANS 12:2 NASB

We find ourselves making decisions based upon a certain belief system. If we are selfish we will make decisions based on what's good for me—not you, not society, not family, but just me. Unfortunately we in America have become a nation all about me! Ever since you were a small child the world has told you how great you are. Even if you can't play baseball, you get a standing ovation when you strike out. We have done away with our grading system and instead everyone is satisfactory. We become teenagers, and our parents say, "You are a selfish young man!" I wonder who has made him that way. As a culture, we all have. In days past, the parents had first priority; not today. It's a child's world. So what does one do to break that cycle? We must be willing to change!

Paul tells us in Romans not to be conformed to the world, but be transformed by the renewing of your mind. Yes, as men, we are constantly battling between being conformed to the world or being transformed by the renewing of our minds.

This is the battle cry: *conformed* vs. *transformed*.

Who is going to win this great battle? How you answer this question will determine who you will become in this earthly life. As your mind thinks, so your actions will be.

The good news is that life is not found in conforming to this world. Let God transform us by the renewing of our minds. Through this transformation He will change the way we think.

> What I believe determines decisions I make and leads me to where I am—actions and outcomes.
>
> —UNKNOWN

When we are transformed by the Holy Spirit we will install God's operating system in our lives.

> Then you will learn to know God's will for you, which is good and pleasing and perfect.
>
> —ROMANS 12:2 NLT

When this battle is won, we begin to change from the "mine" thought to God's will for my life. I begin to think:

- It all belongs to God.
- It all comes from God.
- It is all dispensed by God.

> Whoever it was who searched the heavens with a telescope and found no God would not have found the human mind if he had searched the brain with a microscope.
>
> —GEORGE SANTAYANA

PRAYER: Father God, let me be a man who is willing to change my point of view in life. I want to be a transformed man. Amen.

ACTION: What deeply held beliefs need to be changed in your life? What changes are you willing to make?

REFLECTIONS

It's Good to Be Alone

The sovereign LORD...says: Only in return-
ing to me and waiting for me will you be saved. In
quietness and confidence is your strength.

ISAIAH 30:15 NLT

An American Indian was visiting the big city of New York. As he was strolling along the busy street of Park Avenue, he paused and told his host to be quiet because he heard a cricket. The host asked him how he could hear a cricket with all the noise in the city. The Indian replied, "Because I have learned to hear the cricket when it has been silent in the desert."

We live in such a fast-paced society that we have never taken time to be alone and be where we learn to hear the sounds of nature.

One of the great virtues of the Christian life is learning how to appreciate solitude. As our society gets more technologically advanced, it will become more difficult to be alone. One can't go to a movie anymore without being shaken out of your seat by the loud blasting of special effects. Our music has become so loud that it hurts our ears.

> The state of life is most happy where superfluities are not required and necessities are not wanting.
>
> —PLUTARCH

Many times God's most meaningful touches on our lives come when we are all alone. That is a good thing about illness—it gives us an opportunity to be alone. I have been able to revisit some of the big issues of life while I've laid in my bed. God has provided this quiet time so the two of us can talk. We don't have to wait for illness to occur; schedule time to be alone with God. Take time to go for a long walk in the mountains, in the woods, or by the beach just to be alone with Him. Schedule a time just as you would a business appointment. Some of my most creative times happen when I'm alone with God.

The psalmist writes in Psalm 40:1-3:

> I waited patiently for the LORD, and he inclined to me, and heard my cry. He also brought me up out of a horrible pit, out of the miry clay, and set my feet upon a rock, and established my steps. He has put a new song in my mouth—praise to our God (NKJV).

—◠◡◠—

PRAYER: Father God, my quiet time alone with You is special—I consider it to be very precious to me. Thanks for listening. Amen.

ACTION: Plan a quiet time with God.

REFLECTIONS

Be on the Winning Team

Do you not know that those who run in a race all run, but one receives the prize? Run in such a way that you may obtain it.
1 CORINTHIANS 9:24 NKJV

The world has gone crazy with sports. Twenty-four hours a day, you can view some athletic event—baseball, football, basketball, swimming, soccer, volleyball, and track, to name a few. I can remember when ESPN announced that they were going to create a 24/7 sports channel. I said very prophetically, "There's not enough sports to fill their programming." Boy, was my prophecy off. Any day, any time of the day, there are sporting events shown from around the world. And now, there's even an ESPN2.

Sports on TV are so easily found while we're surfing the channels that we have become knowledgeable about a multitude of different activities. From our armchair, we sometimes think we could accomplish what we watch others do. But the 63 for Tiger Woods or the 42 points for Kobe Bryant, or the three home runs in one game by A-Rod are phenomenal feats that few can duplicate. One of my favorite quotations is:

> The quality of a person's life is in direct proportion to his/her commitment to excellence.
>
> —VINCE LOMBARDI

Paul is a favorite biblical character because he was an outstanding competitor, and he would never quit. What made his career so amazing was that while he was an ardent, follow-the-law Pharisee, he had made it his job to rid the world of Christians. But on his way to Damascus to bring back some of the captured Christians for trial, Paul had a marvelous encounter with God. Paul is the person who penned so many books of the New Testament. He encourages us to run the race to win. In order for us to win the contest, we must deny ourselves many things that would keep us from doing our best. An athlete goes to all the trouble to win the prize, but we do it for a heavenly reward that never disappears.

Paul knew what it took to be a champion. He says that in a race, everyone runs, but only one person wins first prize—so run your race to win. We are all striving to be the people God created us to be and to share God's message of love. Paul's teaching can be rephrased this way:

> If you're going to take the challenge, win.
> We will pay a price to be a winner.

In today's language we would express:

- No pain no gain!
- There is no easy way to success. It's hard work!

Recipe for success:

- Study while others are sleeping.
- Work while other are loafing.
- Prepare while others are playing.
- Dream while others are wishing.

—WILLIAM A. WARD

—◦◦◦—

PRAYER: Father God, give me the excitement needed to run the race to win. I don't want to be just a spectator of life. I want to be a real participant who is willing to pay the price for being a servant to those in need. Amen.

ACTION: Go out and discipline your life for that heavenly reward.

REFLECTIONS

Lost Thankfulness

*For I know the plans that I have for you, declares
the LORD, plans for welfare and not for calamity to give you a future and a hope.*

JEREMIAH 29:11 NASB

We Americans have grown up in an era of abundance. Our minds tell us that life's always going to be good. We yell out, "Let the good times roll." However, at the time of this writing (2009), our economy is suffering a significant downturn. We find that people are losing their jobs and businesses. Many people are seeing a big downturn in their stock portfolios. Inflated home prices are losing value. But here in Southern California, we all still have the same slogan: "No one in Orange County has enough." We want more and we want it now.

We have lost sight of one of God's favorite words—*thankful*. I often say that if we aren't thankful for what we have, we will never be thankful for what we want.

Today's Scripture gives us a hint on how to be thankful in challenging times. Jeremiah states that God's plans are for our welfare and not for calamity, to give us a future and a hope. This means no matter what, God is with us. His Word makes many promises to us regarding Him protecting us in all situations.

- "Oh give thanks to the LORD for He is good; for His loving-kindness is everlasting" (Psalm 106:1 NASB).

- "He gave them their demands but sent them leanness in their souls" (Psalm 106:15 MSG).

- "They found fault with the life they had and turned a deaf ear to God's voice" (Psalm 106:26 MSG).

The consequence of ingratitude is a hardened heart that is not thankful for the slightest blessings.

> Do all things without grumbling or disputing; so that you will prove yourselves to be blameless and innocent, children of God above reproach in the midst of a crooked and perverse generation, among whom you appear as lights in the world.
>
> —Philippians 2:14-15 NASB

This is what a thankful heart does:

- "Always give thanks for everything" (Ephesians 5:20 NLT).

- "In everything give thanks" (1 Thessalonians 5:18 NASB).

- "In everything, by prayer and supplication with thanksgiving let your requests be made known to God" (Philippians 4:6 NASB).

A thankful lifestyle is sweet seasoning to the world. It is a light unto the world. You stand out in a crowd. You will be different.

This thankful lifestyle reflects:

- The password into God's presence is "thank You" (Psalm 100:4).

- Being thankful is a spiritual indicator (Romans 1:21).

- Your way of life reflects that you are satisfied with what you have (1 Thessalonians 5:18). I want what I have, it couldn't be better.

- You have learned to be content whatever the circumstance (Philippians 4:11).

- You may want it, but you don't need it (Psalm 118:24,29).

Praise the LORD, O my soul; all my inmost being, praise his holy name. Praise the LORD, O my soul, and forget not all his benefits.

—Psalm 103:1-2

PRAYER: Father God, I want to be a man who is thankful for all he has. I am content in what I have. You have blessed me beyond any of my expectations. Thank You! Amen.

ACTION: Be a man who gives thanks for all you have; jot ten blessings in your journal.

REFLECTIONS

Feet Like a Deer

*The Lord God is my strength; he will give me the speed
of a deer and bring me safely over the mountains.*
HABAKKUK 3:19 TLB

Deer are such beautiful animals. When I was a young boy, Walt Disney made Bambi come alive. My heart has always been tender to the deer family. They are so agile and run at such speed, even on rough, rocky mountainous terrain.

I am glad just to know that God makes my feet as swift as a deer's and that He enables me to travel safely over higher plains. When our family vacations in the mountains, we love to see the deer on the ridges across the valley. They run with such swiftness, and their lungs are conditioned to race to the highest peak. That's the way I want my life to function.

> The only guide to a man is his conscience; the only shield to his memory is the rectitude and sincerity of his actions.
>
> —WINSTON CHURCHILL

I want to run swiftly toward the mark and run to God's highest calling. I also want my lungs to be so conditioned that I flee with the speed of a deer when I need to run from evil. God's strength is sufficient for my every need.

Just to know that my God is all-knowing (He knows when I must flee and when I must come near) and that He has power over everything gives me assurance. This truth put a stillness in my heart, knowing that He can make my feet run like the feet of a deer.

—✺—

PRAYER: Father God, I trust You to light my path and to turn me around if I'm led into darkness. Amen.

ACTION: Flee from evil with the flashing feet of a deer.

REFLECTIONS

When Bad Times Roll

God is our refuge and strength, always ready to help in times of trouble. So we will not fear when earth-quakes come and the mountains crumble into the sea.

Psalm 46:1-2 nlt

On December 26, 2004, the world was shocked to hear that a 9.3 earth-quake in the ocean off southeast Asia had caused a mighty tsunami to crash ashore in several countries and destroy entire towns, with the death toll at well over 200,000.

People cried out, "Where are You, God? How could You let this happen?" We always ask this "why" question at such times. Why would a loving God permit such death, particularly when the toll included many children?

The sad fact is, we live in a fallen world, and events happen according to the laws of nature. Because of the sin of mankind, there will always be things that happen other than what we would want—a perfect world. There will be troubles and suffering beyond our control. At such times, our comfort must come from God's Word.

In today's verse we find three comforts in such events of life:

- God is our refuge.
- God is our strength.
- God is always ready to help in times of trouble.

If we can internalize these "big three" promises we can live with this victory: We will not live in fear.

What great assurance when our soul quakes. We can apply these promises to all events of life—tsunamis, earthquakes, heartbreaks, or soul quakes.

Just remember, when we walk through life's storms we have two alternatives:

- Respond as a faith-filled person.
- Respond as a faithless person.

How blessed is the man who does not walk in the counsel of the wicked, nor stand in the path of sinners, nor sit in the seat of scoffers! But his delight is in the law of the Lord, and in His law he meditates day and night. He will be like a tree firmly planted by streams of water, which yields its fruit in its season, and its leaf does not wither; and in whatever he does, he prospers (Psalm 1:1-3 NASB).

A faith-filled person will respond in these ways:

- He delights in reading and knowing God's Word.
- He meditates on God's law day and night.
- He will be like a tree firmly planted by streams of water.
- He yields fruit in its season.
- His leaves will not wither.
- He will prosper in all things.

This man of faith understands where he came from and where he is going. He is not one who questions God because of the events of the world. He doesn't look to the world for the answers of life. He is firmly grounded in what God assures him, even when the quakes of life occur.

—∿∿—

PRAYER: Father God, let me stand on Your promises when the quakes of life come my way, as they surely will. Give me the faith to trust Your Word. Amen.

ACTION: Begin today to trust God and all of His promises for you and your family. Reread Psalm 1:2-3.

REFLECTIONS

God Is a Redeemer

I will make up to you for the years that the swarming locust has eaten...You will have plenty to eat and be satisfied and praise the name of the LORD your God.
JOEL 2:25-26 NASB

Look up! Your fields can be restored. The Savior's promise for Israel can also be claimed for your life. Yes, you can even praise God for the locusts of the past. Their devastation is simply a pathway for God to move—and when God moves to restore, He does an awesome job. God renews our past by renewing our present. He gives us new peace, new joy, new goals, new dreams, and new love. What God has promised, He will do.

> Adversity, if for no other reason, is of benefit, since it is sure to bring a season of sober reflection. Men see clearer at such times. Storms purify the atmosphere.
>
> —HENRY WARD BEECHER

In American history, rural farmers have been devastated by the invasion of swarming locusts. Farmers have had to move hundreds of miles, and on occasion, they have had to find a new line of work because the locusts destroyed their way of life.

But God is a God of restoration! Even when the devastation to a human being is like the work of a swarm of locusts on a promising crop—even then, God promises to completely restore everything that has been destroyed.

For five long years when Emilie was going through her chemo, radiation, and bone marrow transplant, we saw little hope of us ever having a normal life again. Our prayers were for that, but her healing was very slow. We looked forward to being able to go to church, go to one of our favorite restaurants, having guests in our home, hugging and shaking hands with our friends. Nothing exciting but just common activities. But now, nine years later, we are back doing all those things. Plus, God has more than redeemed what the locusts had eaten in our life.

Have the locusts eaten anything of yours? Your health, a job, a reputation, a wife, a friend, finances, children? We all have had losses due to the locusts in our lives. Perhaps you have already seen God's restoration and are rejoicing. But you may still be looking out over the fields that were once full and rich with bounty—now destroyed.

Be encouraged and don't give up the fight. You'll be amazed at what God can do. Rose Kennedy expressed it well:

> Birds sing after a storm; why shouldn't people feel free to delight in whatever remains in them.

—〰—

PRAYER: Father God, give me the courage to fight on when I feel that life has been taken away from me! Let me see light at the end of the tunnel. Amen.

ACTION: Pray specifically to God for what the locusts have eaten from your fields.

REFLECTIONS

Four Rules of Hard Labor

Whatever you do, do your work heartily, as for the Lord rather than for men.
COLOSSIANS 3:23 NASB

In America, we seem to be losing a strong labor ethic. The young generation wants to have service people do jobs that the average American male used to do. In Southern California, where I live, I seldom see laborers who are white Americans. If we stopped labor of our immigrants for 24 hours, our cities would come to a standstill. Nothing would get done.

Regardless of gender or nationality, there are four basic principles that one needs to follow:

1. No matter what the task, it's our duty to work for God's glory (Colossians 3:23). In this sense, no job is better than another. Each should result in honor to God.

2. The way we work can earn the respect of those who do not follow Christ (1 Thessalonians 4:11-12). A boss shouldn't have to tell a Christian to use time well or to work hard.

3. Our work is one way to fulfill our dual purpose; to love God and others (Matthew 22:37-40). Showing love to our coworkers is a good way to show that we love God.

4. We must work to provide for those who depend on us (1 Timothy 5:8). Harsh words of criticism are reserved for those who don't take care of their families.[11]

In today's recession, we must take our jobs seriously. We need to thank the Lord each day for a place to work. Having a job is hard work, even for those who enjoy their labors. In the U.S. and Canada, we set aside one day each year to honor our laborers—it's called "Labor Day."

This is a day set aside in both countries to pause and thank those who labor so hard to make our countries productive. We must never underestimate those who provide these services for us.

But until the day comes when our work is over, our task is to make our labor a testimony to God's glory.

> When God wanted sponges and oysters, He made them, and put one on a rock, and the other in the mud. When He made man, He did not make him to be a sponge, or an oyster. He made him with feet and hands, and head, and heart, and vital blood, and a place to use him. "Go work!"
>
> —HENRY WARD BEECHER

PRAYER: Father God, may my work be a form of praise to You. Let me seek Your favor and not those of my boss. Amen.

ACTION: Who are you trying to please with your labor?

REFLECTIONS

A New Heart

*I will give you one heart and a new spirit; I will take from you
your heart of stone and give you tender hearts of love for God.*
EZEKIEL 11:19 TLB

The number one killer for men in America is heart failure. We tend to place tremendous stress upon that pint-sized muscle called the *heart*. Some of the stress on our heart is caused by the food we eat, our high pressure lifestyle, and our lack of physical exercise. Other health problems can stress our hearts as well. And some hearts—such as those with congenital defects—are less able to handle the slightest stress.

> For with the heart a person believes, resulting in righteousness,
> and with the mouth he confesses, resulting in salvation.
> —ROMANS 10:10 NASB

Spiritually speaking, of course, we are all born with a congenital heart problem—*sin*. We are all sinners and prone to rebel against God's plan for our lives. The more we continue on our own way, the more hardened and scarred our spiritual hearts can become. But we don't have to live that way. God promises that He will give us a new heart and a new spirit—without needles or anesthesia. He can replace our hardened old heart with a tender loving one.

To take advantage of this wonderful opportunity, all you have to do is surrender your heart to Him. Why wait?

You shall love the Lord your God with all your heart, and with all your soul, and with all your mind, and with all your strength.

—Mark 12:30 nasb

PRAYER: Father God, our confidence is based in Your Word. Your Word is true. Let wisdom reign in my life as I put my trust in You. Amen.

ACTION: Tell someone about your new heart.

REFLECTIONS

The Strength to Change

If anyone is in Christ, he is a new creation;
the old has gone, the new has come!
2 CORINTHIANS 5:17

They say that you can't teach an old dog to change, but I want to tell you that's not true. In fact, if you do something for 21 consecutive days, you can create a new habit. We as individuals must realize that we no longer want to be as we have been, but since knowing Jesus, I realize that I no longer like my old self.

Becoming a man of God begins with making a personal commitment to Jesus Christ. Only He can give us the strength to change. Only He can give us the fresh start that allows the spirit to grow strong in us.

Second Corinthians 5:17 reminds us, "If anyone is in Christ, he is a new creation; the old has gone, the new has come!" That's what I discovered many years ago. My life began to change from that moment on, and the years since then have always been an exciting adventure.

> Lazy people finally die of hunger because they won't get up and go to work. Sinners are always wanting what they don't have; the God-loyal are always giving what they do have.
>
> —PROVERBS 21:25-26 MSG

It hasn't always been easy. I've had to give up much bitterness, anger, fear, hatred, and resentment. Many times I've had to back up and start over, asking God to take over control of my life and show me His way to live.

But as I have learned to follow Him, He has guided me through times of pain and joy, struggle, and growth. And how rewarding it has been to see growth take root and grow in my life. I give thanks and praise for all His goodness to me over the years.

I'm not finished yet—far from it. Growing in godliness is a lifelong process. Although God is the One who makes it possible, He requires my cooperation. If I want to be more like God and to have this shine in my life and in my home, I must be willing to change what God wants me to change and learn what He wants to teach me.

PRAYER: Father God, I realize that change is possible. Give me the strength to change more like You! Amen.

ACTION: In your journal list three things you want to change about yourself. Then beside each one state what you are gong to do to make that change possible.

REFLECTIONS

Be Thankful and Content in All Things

Bless the LORD, O my soul; and all that is within
me, bless His holy name. Bless the LORD, O
my soul, and forget none of His benefits.
PSALM 103:1-2 NASB

One of the greatest expressions in the English language is *thank you*. At an early age, we begin to teach our children to say these two magical words. When someone gives them a gift or compliment—and before they can even utter the words—we jump right in and remind them, "Now what do you say?" However, as we grow from childhood to adulthood, we often forget our manners and hold back from expressing our appreciation to someone who does us a service.

It's the same way with God. He loves to hear and know we are thankful for all He bestows upon us. He is a provider of all we have.

> There is nothing better for a man than to eat and drink and tell himself that his labor is good. This also I have seen that it is from the hand of God. For who can eat and who can have enjoyment without Him?
>
> —ECCLESIASTES 2:24-25 NASB

Thankful hearts give thanks. One way to express our thanks for our food is to give a blessing each time we have a meal. Our family always gives a blessing of grace before we eat. This is a tradition at home or out at a restaurant.

We never want to forget where our food comes from. We always want to let God know that we appreciate His providing us our food.

As I've gotten older, I look back over this short life and realize that God has been faithful along the way. He has always provided for all our needs. Not necessarily for our wants but for our needs. That is totally in keeping with the words found in 2 Peter 1:3:

> His divine power has granted to us everything pertaining to life and godliness, through the true knowledge of Him who called us by His own glory and excellence (NASB).

The password for entering into God's presence is "thank You."

> Enter His gates with thanksgiving, and His courts with praise, give thanks to Him; bless His name.
>
> —PSALM 100:4

We humbly reach out to God with thanksgiving and praise. One of the leading indicators of our spiritual walk with God is our thankfulness for all He has done for us.

Paul wrote that he had learned to be content in all situations (Philippians 4:11). When we are restless and find ourselves discontent with our lives and our situations, it's accentuated when we don't have a heart that really gives thanks.

———

PRAYER: Father God, don't let me forget to always be thankful for what You do for me. You are a gracious God who continually pours out blessings on my life. Thank You for everything—big and small. Amen.

ACTION: Evaluate the thankfulness of your heart. How could it be improved?

REFLECTIONS

Ten Good Friends

A cord of three strands is not quickly torn apart.
ECCLESIASTES 4:12 NASB

Here's an interesting story to consider:

"I wish I had some good friends to help me in life!" cried lazy Dennis. "Good friends? Why, you have ten!" replied his master. "I'm sure I don't have half that many, and those I have are too poor to help me." "Count your fingers, my boy," said his master. Dennis looked down at his strong hands. "Count thumbs and all," added the master. "I have; there are ten," replied the lad. "Then never say you don't have ten good friends to help you on in life. Try what those true friends can do before you grumble and fret because you do not get help from others."[12]

Many times we look to others to help us out, and we complain when we don't receive the help we think we deserve. But help starts within ourselves. Then it moves outward. In the Christian community, we often hear this advice: "Let go, let God." This sounds good upon first hearing it, but in reality we should be saying, "I'll do my part and let God do His part." God doesn't want us to sit back and not do our part. We need to take an inventory of all the skills and tools that God has so graciously given us at birth. We tend to take for granted those attributes of success which were given us at the very beginning of our life. Our fingers and thumbs are such valuable tools for work. They truly are our dearest friends.

King Solomon in all his wisdom told us that friends are great blessings to our family. He emphasized these principles in Ecclesiastes 4:

- Two are better than one because they have a good return for their labor (verse 9).
- Woe to the one who falls when there is not another to lift him up (verse 10).
- When two lie down together they keep warm (verse 11).
- Two can resist one who tries to overpower them (verse 12).
- A cord of three strands is not quickly torn apart (verse 12).

When you seem to be down and when things aren't going your way, take a piece of paper and a pencil in hand and jot down all the blessings God has given you. Pretty soon you will realize that you are a very blessed man—you have family, friends, a job, a home, a car, etc. One of your most valuable assets in life are your ten fingers—take good care of them because they are very valuable tools to bring you out of the pit.

> So much unhappiness, it seems to me, is due to nerves; and bad nerves are the result of having nothing to do, or doing a thing badly, unsuccessfully or incompetently. Of all the unhappy people in the world, the unhappiest are those who have not found something they want to do. True happiness comes to him who does his work well, followed by a relaxing, a refreshing period of rest. True happiness comes from the right amount of work for the day.
>
> —Lin Yutang

PRAYER: Father God, let me realize the resources I have in my hands. If You do Your part, I'm willing to do mine. Thanks for Your help. Amen.

ACTION: Count your blessings and name them one by one.

REFLECTIONS

Hear the Bells

*Ascribe to the LORD the glory due to His
name; worship the LORD in holy array.*
PSALM 29:2 NASB

A young man from a west Texas farm community received a football scholarship from a small college in Texas. He was very excited about his new adventures. After he had packed his bags to take to school, his mother said goodbye. After her hugs and tears, she asked her son to make her one promise. "Be sure to attend church every Sunday while you are away from home." With no hesitation, he assured his mama he would honor that request.

After settling into his dorm, he met several incoming freshmen he liked. However, these young men had few if any spiritual interests. One of the boys came from a wealthy farm family nearby, and he invited his new friends to come home with him for the weekend to hunt and fish. Of course, this small town farm boy said, "Yes, that will be fun."

On Sunday morning as they were mounting up on their horses to take them where the hunting and fishing were good, the young man heard the loud bell ring from a nearby church. They rode on farther toward their day's adventure when again the young man heard a fainter ringing of the church bell. Going farther toward their destination and farther from the church bell, this young man again heard the church bell ring, but this time the sound was very faint. He stopped his horse and told his host he had to go back and attend church. The host said, "We don't have to go to church today. Let's go on and I will go to church with you next week." The young man replied, "No, I must go back while I can still hear the bell."

Are you in that young man's position? Maybe you once heard God's strong voice, but today you have moved away from God. His voice is no longer strong but has become fainter and fainter. Your conscience might be calling out, "Go back while you can still hear the voice of God!"

If you feel far away from God, guess who moved? Return to Him before you no longer hear His voice calling you to come back home.

—⁓—

PRAYER: Father God, continue to ring the bell loud and clear. I never want to stop hearing your call. May everything that would hinder me from hearing Your voice be silenced. Amen.

ACTION: How clear do you hear the bell ring? If it's not clear, you will want to turn back again to your first love.

REFLECTIONS

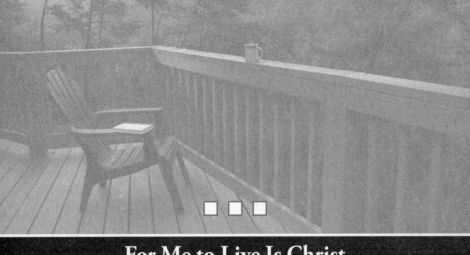

For Me to Live Is Christ

Even though the fig trees are all destroyed, and there is neither blossom left nor fruit; though the olive crops all fail, and the fields lie barren; even if the flocks die in the fields and the cattle barns are empty, yet I will rejoice in the LORD; I will be happy in the God of my salvation.

HABAKKUK 3:17-18 TLB

We live in a world that measures success by our titles, trophies, toys, and salary. We have value if we have accumulated a lot of things. In reading Solomon's journey in life as shared in the book of Ecclesiastes, we are exposed to what his reply was regarding his possession: "Vanity of vanities! All is vanity" (Ecclesiastes 1:2 NASB).

> Thus I considered all my activities which my hands had done and the labor which I had exerted, and behold all was vanity and striving after the wind and there was no profit under the sun.
>
> —ECCLESIASTES 2:11 NASB

As Solomon gave witness too, many times as we look back, we see that most of our possessions have faded away. Health becomes so precious when we no longer have it. Paul expresses it very well when he says:

> For me, to live is Christ and to die is gain.
>
> —PHILIPPIANS 1:21

Paul understood the ultimate principle for successful living. He realized

149

that though our material possessions can be wonderful and enjoyable, the real joys that last forever are our steadfast trust and joy in the Lord. Through good times and bad times, through sickness and health, through the up times and down times, we need to express joy—because God has saved us from our sins.

Job responded to his wife by reflecting what his priorities were toward God. Job's wife asked him why he didn't curse God and die (Job 2:9). And Job gave a great declaration of his faith when he said, "Shall we indeed accept good from God and not accept adversity?" (verse 10).

Job was stripped of every possession that he had, all his family, his barns, and his livestock, yet he stated, "For me to live is Christ." Ultimately God restored to Job all that the locusts had eaten.

> The Lord restored the fortunes of Job when he prayed for his friends, and the Lord increased all that Job had twofold.
>
> Job 42:10 NASB

Can we as men stand before God and call out, "For me to live is Christ"?

—∿∿—

PRAYER: Father God, give me the faith that I might be able to say with excitement and dedication, "For me to live is Christ."

ACTION: Take inventory of your life and see how it measures up to your commitment.

REFLECTIONS

Born Again

> *Man looks on the outward appear-*
> *ance, but the Lord looks on the heart.*
> 1 SAMUEL 16:7 AMP

Reality TV is the latest fad in television production. We have all seen them. Think of those extreme makeover programs that are recreating rooms, homes, yards, and even individuals. That's right. Individuals. And women aren't the only ones who can get caught up in this. We men often desire changes in our bodies too.

One such program is titled the "Million Dollar Makeover." When I first heard about the show, I thought to myself, "What does one get for a million dollars?" They promised to transform people into their idea of the perfect human being. A man or woman could undergo any drastic change he or she desired. When they were through with you, you would be a fake person. You couldn't even recognize yourself.

As I leaned back on the sofa, I realized that altering my physical appearance would not change the real me because I reflected on today's Scripture: "Man looks on the outward appearance, but the Lord looks on the heart."

In John 3:1-21, Jesus is in deep conversation with a Pharisee named Nicodemus, ruler of the Jews, and is explaining the need for his heart to be remade. Jesus explained to Nicodemus that an outward appearance of devotion was simply not enough.

In the conversation that follows, Nicodemus finally asks Jesus the all-important question, "How can a man be born again when he is old? He cannot enter a second time into his mother's womb and be born, can he?" (verse 4 NASB).

Jesus went on to tell this Pharisee that he must be born both of the flesh and the spirit. Now that is the ultimate transformation.

You might be asking the same question in life. Inside your soul and heart, you are yearning for a peace that you aren't experiencing in your everyday life. You look into the mirror, and your physical body looks okay, but there are unsatisfied tensions upon your inner self.

> There is nothing more certain in TIME or ETERNITY than what Jesus Christ did on the Cross. He switched the whole of the human race back into right relationship with God. He made Redemption the basis of human life, that is, he made a way for every son/daughter of man to get into communion with God. The center of salvation is the Cross of Jesus, and the reason it is so easy to obtain salvation is because it cost God so much.
>
> —OSWALD CHAMBERS

If you find yourself in the same situation as Nicodemus, you might go to Romans 10:9-10 and find out how to be born again. It says:

> If you confess with your mouth, "Jesus is Lord," and believe in your heart that God raised Him from the dead, you will be saved. For it's with your heart that you believe and are justified, and it is with your mouth that you confess and are saved.

—◦◦◦—

PRAYER: Father God, don't let me get caught up in the world's thought pattern which declares that I should drastically change my physical appearance. Let me be satisfied with how You have created me. Let me concentrate on my inner-qualities that they become more Christ like. Amen.[13]

ACTION: In your journal list those qualities of Christ's which you want to become. Work on *this* change.

REFLECTIONS

On Bended Knee

I have learned to be content in whatever circumstances I am.
PHILIPPIANS 4:11 NASB

In 1997, there were two deaths that brought world attention; one was Princess Diana and the other was Mother Teresa. There was also another death, which hardly received any notice. That was the death of an Austrian psychiatrist by the name of Viktor Frankl, who died on September 2 at the age of 93.

During World War II, Dr. Frankl was put in prison at Auschwitz, where he became a common laborer and not the world class doctor of psychiatry. He was there as a prisoner of the German army and not as a noted doctor. Much of his family, his father, his mother, his brother, and his wife died in this hellhole of a prison.

The Nazis destroyed all of his lifelong research and notes which filled many journals. Through all this he came from Auschwitz believing that "everything can be taken from a man but one thing; the last of the human freedoms—to choose one's attitude in any given set of circumstances."

> We can respond to the difficulties in life by raising a clenched
> fist or on a bended knee—you choose.
>
> —KENTON BESHORE

We may not be able to choose our circumstances in life, but we can choose what our attitude will be. The apostle Paul gave us an example of how this works. He wrote in Philippians 4:11,13:

155

I have learned to be content in whatever circumstances I am...
I can do all things through Him who strengthens me (NASB).

Whatever our circumstances may be, we can draw on the power of Jesus for the strength to face them. We have the freedom to choose which way we will respond—either being content, or to raise a clinched fist heavenward.

I am always content with what happens; for I know that what God chooses is better than what I choose.

—EPICTETUS

PRAYER: Father God, I keep on learning to forget the anger when things don't go right. I've learned to look up and ask, "Lord, what are You trying to teach me through this trial?"

ACTION: Go to God on your bended knee.

REFLECTIONS

Becoming the Salt of Life

We are a fragrance of Christ to God among
those who are being saved...
2 CORINTHIANS 2:15 NASB

The Scriptures tell us that we (Christians) are the salt of the earth (Matthew 5:13). We give hope to the world. Where would the world be without the fragrance of the Christian church? Most hospitals were founded by the followers of Jesus. The same could be said of our universities, our libraries, and our relief efforts. So is salt good or bad? This is not an easy question to answer. On one hand, it is good. On the other hand, it is bad. For instance, the same salt is used to clear the roadways of ice and snow, but it also causes the rust to eat holes in the metal of automobiles. The salt is one of the leading causes of high blood pressure, but is also used to help athletes from losing too much liquid and thus becoming dehydrated.

Salt is like a gun—there is a little good news and a little bad news. As we learn more about what the Scriptures of the Bible say about a particular topic, we grow in our understanding of how to apply this information to our daily lives. Thus the Word will change who we are, the choices we make, and how we treat people.

As great as salt is to the believing world, it is very destructive to those who reject Jesus.

> For we are a fragrance of Christ to God among those who are being saved and among those who are perishing; to the one an

aroma from death to death, to the other an aroma from life to life.

—2 Corinthians 2:15-16 nasb

The same gospel brings life to the believer and death to the rejecter. Jesus, our Savior, is merciful and patient to those who call upon Him in faith, but He is also Judge, whose anger rests upon those who spitefully refuse to bow down to Him as their Lord.

It's important that we grow in Jesus so we can be a refreshing fragrance to those who are lost in this very confusing life. If we don't stand for something, we won't stand for anything.

As your life reflects the peace and patience of the Lord, you reflect that to those who are around you. They will be attracted to you.

> Amazing grace! how sweet the sound!
> That saved a wretch like me!
> I once was lost, but now am found;
> Was blind, but now I see.
>
> 'Twas grace that taught my heart to fear,
> And grace my fears relieved.
> How precious did that grace appear
> The hour I first believed!
>
> Thro' many dangers, toils, and snares
> I have already come.
> 'Tis grace hath bro't me safe thus far,
> And grace will lead me home.
>
> —John Newton

—◦◦◦—

PRAYER: Father God, may my salt be for good to those who are around me. May others see You through my life. May I be the salt of the world! Amen.

ACTION: Does your life melt ice from the highway, or does it cause rust on metal?

REFLECTIONS

Who Gives You Comfort?

Thy rod and thy staff they comfort me.
PSALM 23:4 KJV

We are living in an age when no one wants to have discomfort. The slightest pain and we want a pill to make our hurt go away. We have an emotional crisis and we seek out professional help. Our finances go astray and we are devastated. What do we do when these emergencies come to us? Most Americans will quickly seek something that will deaden the pain. It might be a pill, a drug, a liquid, an injection, an escape—anything to get us out of our problems.

There is a better alternative and that is what the psalmist gives in the fourth verse of the famous twenty-third psalm: "Thy rod and thy staff, they comfort me" (KJV).

The shepherd protects his sheep with his rod or club, which is used to fight off wild beasts, and he guides straying sheep with his staff and crook. The great English preacher Charles Spurgeon reflects on this great comfort:

> Give me the comforts of God, and I can well bear the taunts of men. Let me lay my head on the bosom of Jesus, and I fear not the distraction of care and trouble. If my God will give the light of His smile, and grant His benediction, it is enough. Come on foes, persecutors...the Lord God is my sun and shield...I carry a sun within; blow, wind of the frozen north, I have a fire of living coal within; yea, death, slay me, but I have another life—a life in the light of God's countenance.

Here was a man who knew that Jesus was all he needed. He was secure in his faith and realized that his comfort came from the rod and staff of his Shepherd—Jesus Christ.

Take a look at your daily newspaper or TV news and you will realize how various people try to comfort their discomfort. You will realize that we face ongoing problems of violence, life-threatening disease, and political uncertainty every day.

The challenge of the Christian is to live in the world but not by its standards. To live by the world's standards is to have the world's strength in the day of trouble. To live by God's grace is to have God's strength in the day of trouble.

> Faith is an act of rational choice which determines us to act as if certain things were true and in confident expectation that they will prove to be true.
>
> —WILLIAM R. INGE

—◦◦◦—

PRAYER: Father God, through the years You have protected and guided me with Your rod and staff. You have held me up in times of weakness. I appreciate the strength and comfort You have given me. Amen.

ACTION: Be a comforter to someone today.

REFLECTIONS

God Is Bound by His Promises

Keep watching and praying that you may not enter into
temptation; the spirit is willing, but the flesh is weak.
MATTHEW 26:41 NASB

G od always keeps His promises. His character will not let Him fall back. In truth, all prayers offered through His Son, Jesus, are bound to be heard. God finds joy in keeping His promises.

God's actions are always consistent with His character, including His love, righteousness, holiness, and justice. He cannot lay aside any one of His attributes and act independently of it. It is part of His being to be just. In all of His actions, God acts with fairness. If He did less, He would no longer be God.

> The Rock! His work is perfect, for all His ways are just; a God of faithfulness and without injustice, righteous and upright is He.
>
> —DEUTERONOMY 32:4 NASB

We live in a day where all aspects of life are being undermined by dishonesty. Families have lost most of their retirement funds because they believed executives' promises that were made with their fingers crossed behind their backs.

Oh, how desperate our country is for people with character! We look to our sport heroes, our political leaders, our corporate leadership, the stars of movies and television, and even our spiritual leaders, hoping they will show us how people of character live. Each time we feel comfortable that a certain personality has the answer, we are disappointed by some revelation of broken dreams and promises.

We expect people to do what they say they are going to do. We are disappointed when a plumber, an electrician, a painter, or a coworker can't do what they've said they are going to do. They miss the appointment or don't deliver their product on time—and here we patiently wait and nothing happens. Even parents tell their children that such-and-such will happen on Saturday, and it doesn't happen as promised. How many children go to their rooms to cry because a promise is broken?

We are so thankful we have One who never goes back on His promises. God the Father, Jesus the Son, and the Holy Spirit always keep their word. If they said it, you can believe it. Let's all learn from the Master of character to "just do what you say you are going to do."

———

PRAYER: Father God, thanks for being a promise-keeper. You are the model for every man who wants to be an honorable man. You give great confidence from Your Word because I know You won't break Your promise. If You said it, I believe it. Amen.

ACTION: Make and keep a promise to someone today—even a small one. Make this practice a discipline of your faith.

REFLECTIONS

Acquire a Discerning Heart

*Give your servant a discerning heart to govern your
people and to distinguish between right and wrong.*
1 KINGS 3:9

One of the confusions we have in today's culture is how do we tell right from wrong. No one wants to be brave enough to call a spade a spade. We don't want to hurt anyone's feelings or look like we are out on the fringes.

> An English theologian tells the story of a young man who went to college. When he had been there a year his father asked him, "What do you know? Do you know more than when you went?" "Oh, yes!" he replied. "I do."
>
> Then he went the second year, and was asked the same question: "Do you know more than when you went?" "Oh, no!" he replied; "I know a great deal less." "Well," said the father, "you are making progress."
>
> Then he went the third year, and was asked, "What do you know now?" "Oh!" he replied, "I don't think I know anything." "That's right," said the father; "you have now learned to profit, since you say you know nothing."
>
> He who is convinced that he knows nothing of himself as he ought to know gives up steering his ship and lets God put his hand on the rudder. He lays aside his own wisdom and cries

out, "O God, my little wisdom is cast at Your feet; my little judgment is given to You."[14]

Solomon must have been similar to this young college student, for he too knew the wisdom of being humble when it came to leading the people he had inherited from his father, King David. In his dream God asked Solomon, "Ask for whatever you want me to give you" (2 Chronicles 1:7). Solomon in all of his youth (about 20 years old) declared with great wisdom, "Give me wisdom and knowledge, that I may lead this people, for who is able to govern this great people of yours?" (2 Chronicles 1:10).

What a great declaration to know that by his own power he wasn't qualified to lead and to govern his people! He also wanted to know right from wrong.

As a dad, do you hear the simple humility of such a great man of God? If he didn't feel confident in his task, is it any wonder that sometimes we are dismayed at trying to lead our children properly? If Solomon could so humbly face God and ask Him such a simple request, why should we feel at a loss when we too feel helpless?

> Ideas not coupled with action never become bigger than the brain cells they occupied.
>
> —Arnold H. Glascow

We need to approach God as a servant, one who realizes that only through the power and guidance from God can he do anything. We, as men, aren't capable under our own strength.

———

PRAYER: Father God, give me a discerning heart. I want to be able to know right from wrong, and I also want to be able to teach that to my children. Amen.

ACTION: Share with a buddy that you would like to be held accountable for having a discerning heart.

REFLECTIONS

Hurry, Hurry, Hurry

*Man is never so tall as when he kneels before God—never
so great as when he humbles himself before God. And
the man who kneels to God can stand up to anything.*

Louis H. Evans

Faster, faster, faster.

I'm always on the go, and you probably are too. Technology, marvelous as it may be, hasn't done a thing to ease our pace. In fact, it has pushed us harder and faster. The faster I move, the more someone wants and expects me to take it up yet another notch. I'm certain this is not what God had in mind when He created us. As His children, we need to fight the urge to be swept along in this hurry-up mentality.

So what's the alternative? Becoming castaways on a tropical island? Getting rid of our computers and cell phones? No, if we're to function effectively, we must find a healthy balance. Living in hyperdrive may not be God's will, but neither is checking out of life and collecting cobwebs. I remember reading something Chuck Swindoll said years ago: "The zealot says, 'I would rather burn out than rust out!' But what's the difference? Either way you're out!"

Again, there must be balance, a *moderation* (my family's favorite word). In order to accomplish this equilibrium, I've learned to pray on my feet or—to say it another way—to pray on the go.

From one end to the other, Scripture gives us examples of where and how to pray:

- "Pray without ceasing" (1 Thessalonians 5:17 NASB).

- "Call upon Me in the day of trouble; I shall rescue you" (Psalm 50:15 NASB).

- "Pour out your heart before Him; God is a refuge for us" (Psalm 62:8 NASB).

- "Seek the LORD while He may be found; call upon Him while He is near" (Isaiah 55:6 NASB).

- "Ask, and it will be given you; seek, and you will find; knock, and it will be opened to you" (Matthew 7:7 NASB).

One of the main purposes of faith is to bring us into direct, personal, vital contact with the living God. When we pray, we admit our profound need, our helplessness to do life without Him. Even though God knows all of our daily needs, our praying for them changes our attitude from complaints and criticism to praise. In some real-but-mysterious way, praying allows us to participate in God's personal plan for our lives.

Jesus taught His disciples that "at all times they ought to pray and not lose heart" (Luke 18:1 NASB). Even though answers to prayer don't always come along immediately, we should not be discouraged...or stop praying! Oh, how my family had to learn these things as we prayed fervently for God to heal Emilie's cancer. We wanted an immediate healing that would have the medical profession declaring, "It's a miracle!" Instead we had to learn time and again that God's timetable was not our own.[15]

> Be still, and know that I am God.
>
> —PSALM 46:10

—⁓⁓—

PRAYER: Father God, let me slow down and let me spend more time in Your presence. I know that prayer gives me strength to get through the day. Amen.

ACTION: Start today to spend time with God.

REFLECTIONS

Check Your Power Source

The Lord says, "I will make my people strong with power from me!...Wherever they go they will be under my personal care."
ZECHARIAH 10:12 TLB

One morning while preparing breakfast, Emilie put two pieces of bread in the toaster, pushed down the level, walked away to soft boil her eggs, and returned in a few minutes to find her bread still in the toaster—but not toasted. She scratched her head, pushed down the lever once again, but this time she didn't walk away—she stayed close by to observe what went wrong the first time. Again no toast and no hot wires visible to toast her bread. "Why oh why?" she asked. "Why isn't my bread toasting?"

Over her shoulder I uttered, "Have you ever thought of plugging the cord into the socket?" She then realized her mistake—she couldn't get toast if the toaster wasn't plugged in to the power source. We don't get answers from God when we're not plugged into Him.

In Southern California where I live, we have many service companies that want to take care of my every need. We have personal trainers, personal shoppers, home decorators, personal animal groomers, valet parking, and personal guides for our amusement parks. However, none of these services can take care of our spiritual needs. We need someone much larger in life than a service provider.

Since God has promised to make us strong with His power source, we need to break out and take some control over our lives. God has given us many truths that enable us to make appropriate choices for proper and healthy living.

When we are confronted with certain illnesses (as many of us are) we must rely on good common sense. Your intuition will give you insight on what needs to be done. Just make sure you are plugged into the right power source.

Remember that God is always there looking over your shoulder. When He is needed, He is there! You are under His personal care at all times.

———

PRAYER: Father God, let me rely on Your power more. The weight that I'm personally carrying is too heavy. Help me to say "no" when I find myself trying to solve all my problems. Amen.

ACTION: Go to God in prayer for your decisions. Depend upon Him more each day. Step down so He can step up.

REFLECTIONS

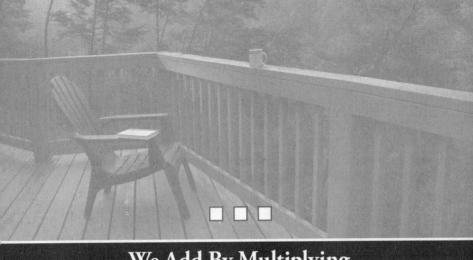

We Add By Multiplying

By this My Father is glorified that you bear much fruit; so you will be my disciples.
JOHN 15:8 NKJV

In elementary school we learn to add first, then by third grade we learn our multiplication tables. In essence we find out that multiplication is really a fast way to add. An example of this would be, What is the sum of 5 x 4? We could add

4	
4	
4	or we could multiply
4	5
4	x4
20	20

That's the way in bearing fruit to the Lord. We could bear fruit over a long period of time, or by multiplying—which brings many at one time.

A few years ago, the Museum of Science and Industry in Chicago had a fascinating display. It showed a checkerboard with one grain of wheat on the first square, 2 on the second, 4 on the third, then 8, 16, 32, 64, and so on until they could no longer fit the seeds on the square. Then it asked the question, "At this rate of doubling each successive square, how much would you have on the checkerboard by the sixty-fourth square?"

You could punch a button at the bottom of the display to find out. The answer? "Nine sextillion—enough grain to cover the entire subcontinent of India 50 feet deep." Amazing!

If each one of us would lead just one person to Christ each year, and each of those persons leads one to Christ each year, the harvest would soon be enormous. We should be encouraged to share Jesus' good news. If we bring even one person to the Lord, and that one brings one, and so on, there is great potential for multiplying just as a planted seed reproduces.

> Anyone can devise a plan by which good people may go to Heaven. Only God can devise a plan whereby sinners, who are His enemies, can go to Heaven.
>
> —Lewis Sperry Chafer

PRAYER: Father God, may I have the zeal to share my faith in You with others I meet. May others see You in me. Amen.

ACTION: Read John, chapter 7: the importance of abiding in Christ.

REFLECTIONS

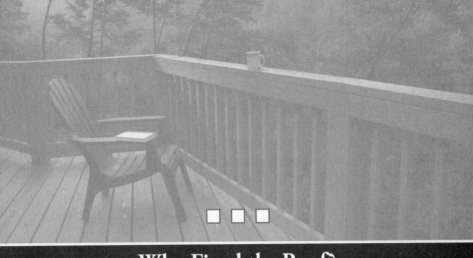

Who Fixed the Roof?

*He said to the paralytic—"I say to you, get up, and
pick up your stretcher and go home."*
LUKE 5:24 NASB

The setting for this story opens with some friends of a crippled man who want to bring him to Jesus to be healed. The sick man couldn't walk, so they carried him on his personal bed. Can you imagine how the people of the city stared as they watched a man being carried on his bed to see Jesus? As the group arrived at the home where Jesus was teaching, they saw a large crowd of people and couldn't even get close to Jesus for the healing of their friend.

One of the friends said, "Let's go over the crowd and take him upon the roof." Then they climbed up some outside stairs with the sick man on his bed. They reasoned that they had to take off some of the flat roof to lower the man and his bed inside the home near Jesus. I can just hear the dialogue that went on between the friends:

- This will be fun—like a party.
- We can't tear into a roof.
- The debris will fall down on top of Jesus.
- Who will fix the roof when we're finished?

Fortunately for the sick man, someone took control and started taking off a section of the roof. Then they tied ropes to the corners of the bed and let the man and his bed down through the hole in the roof.

You can imagine the amazement that Jesus and those in the crowd experienced as they saw a man and bed being lowered through the roof. Some could have thought:

- The nerve of them.
- Can't they take their turn?
- Gate crashers—go to the back of the line.
- Escort them out!
- Make them wait in line and take their turn like we did.

But Jesus looked at the man who had come down through the roof. Then He smiled and said, "Your sins are forgiven."

Some of the scribes and Pharisees (Jewish leaders) were very upset. "Who does this Jesus think He is? Only God can forgive a man's sins!"

But Jesus replied, "You're right. Only God can forgive sins. I will show you that I can forgive sins." So He turned to the sick man and said, "Rise and take up your stretcher and go home."

At once, the paralytic man rose up before them all and took up his bed and went home glorifying God.

> The difference between perseverance and obstinacy is that one often comes from a strong will and the other from a strong won't.
>
> —Henry Ward Beecher

Fortunately, the friends hadn't spent time debating who would fix the roof. They just earnestly wanted to get their friend healed. Jesus also was open to the very unorthodox way in which the sick man was brought to Him, and the sick man was obedient to Jesus' command when He said, "Stand and walk."

The Bible clearly commands us to always obey the Lord (Acts 5:29; Daniel 7:27). In James 1:22 we are specifically required to hear His Word and to do His will. We should be obedient to God because of our love for Him (1 John 2:3-4). These acts are to be a reflection of the inner reality that we truly love the Lord and are committed to His ways.

Do we care enough for a friend of ours that we would be willing to bring them to hear Jesus? That is a big question. How much do you love your friends? Or do you sit back and ask the question, "But who will fix the roof?"

Those who bring sunshine to the lives of others cannot keep it from themselves.

—Unknown

—⁓—

PRAYER: Father God, may I be willing to bring a friend to Jesus. I want my heart to ache for my friends who do not know who You are. Amen.

ACTION: Can you think of a friend who needs to be lowered through the roof?

REFLECTIONS

Secrets for Financial Strength

Where money speaks the truth is silent.
RUSSIAN PROVERB

Money is a big mystery! Many people spend their whole lives working for it, and some even die for it, but many aren't happy with it when they get it. Money is like a gun; in the right hands it can be a tool for justice; in the hands of a criminal it can become a weapon of evil.

Really, money is simply a commodity for exchange. It enables us to provide a means to an end—the purchase of something. There are four ways in which we get money:

- We can work for it.

- We can loan it to someone else and earn interest on it.

- We can subcontract it out to someone else and earn a profit from his or her labor.

- We can invest it (risk it) in order to speculate that we may earn a profit.

There are many experts in the field of Christian money management, most of whom give different formulas and principles on how to use God's resources of money. Emilie and I have adopted four basic guidelines or secrets to assist us in handling money and developing a sound money-managing strategy.

Secret One: Earn Little by Little

The writer of Proverbs understood earning very well for he wrote in Proverbs 13:11, "Wealth obtained by fraud dwindles, but the one who gathers by labor increases it" (NASB). The NIV reads, "He who gathers money little by little makes it grow." That's the basic concept behind accumulation of excess money beyond the monthly expenses. The Lord rewards those who are patient and content with their lives. The prize doesn't always go to the swift. Develop a life of being satisfied with a little at a time.

Secret Two: Save Little by Little

America is a spending country, but we must turn to becoming a saving country if we are to survive financially. One of the greatest services you can give your children is to teach them how to save on a regular basis. Saving for retirement seems to be on everyone's mind. Even young people think about this great benchmark in life. You need to start early to save for your children's education and for your retirement.

Here are several ways to achieve this goal:

- Open an IRA or a Roth IRA account with your bank or any reputable investment broker.
- Contribute to your retirement plan at work.
- Invest in a reputable no-load mutual fund.
- Invest in companies which permit you to reinvest with dividends that are earned.
- Don't take out interest and dividends earned; reinvest again.
- Purchase rental income on a regular basis.
- Interview and select a good investment counselor who will assist you in these areas if you are a beginner.

This principle of saving little by little helps develop good Christian character qualities of diligence, industry, prudence, and patience. A small amount of money saved regularly grows faster than the average person realizes.

Secret Three—Share Your Blessings

If you live within these basic principles, you will be able to share with others a part of what God has so richly given you.

- Give to your local church.
- Give to other parachurch organizations.
- Give to local community needs.
- Give to individuals who have needs.
- Give to missions, etc.

Secret Four—Stay Out of Debt

The advertising industry, along with manufacturers of products, have conditioned us to BUY—BUY—BUY. We are a consumer nation, and the economic policy that stimulates this mind-set is called consumerism. Romans 12:2 comes to mind, because we truly are in a war of either conforming to the world system or of us being transformed by the renewing of our minds.

The way most of us can get ahead to a bigger-than-life scenario is to charge on our credit cards. This is not good. We must learn to live within our means. Since our culture says, "The man who dies with the most toys wins," we have to discipline ourselves not to go into more debt than we can afford with our present income.

Debt is the very opposite of savings. In life we either earn interest or we pay interest. The wisdom of Proverbs speaks specifically about staying out of debt:

- "Better is he who is lightly esteemed and has a servant than he who honors himself and lacks bread" (Proverbs 12:9 NASB).

- "There is one who pretends to be rich, but has nothing; another pretends to be poor; but has great wealth" (Proverbs 13:7 NASB).

Credit cards are the "genies in the glass bottle" that let us enter into the world of make-believe. They let us buy products we can't afford. Improper use of credit cards (debt) will prevent you from managing your money properly.

Here are some other teachings in Scripture:

- "No one can serve two masters. For you will hate one and love the other, or be devoted to one and despise the other. You cannot serve both God and money" (Matthew 6:24).

- "A faithful man will abound with blessings" (Proverbs 28:20 NASB).

- "Wise people think before they act, fools don't and even brag about it" (Proverbs 13:16 NASB).

- "Seek first His kingdom and His righteousness, and all these things will be added to you" (Matthew 6:33 NASB).

- "Owe nothing to anyone except to love one another" (Romans 13:8 NASB).

You will not have financial freedom as long as the monster of debt controls your life. Here are some remedies for overuse of credit cards:

- Use your credit card to your advantage, and not to the advantage of the lender.

- Pay off the balance owed at the end of each monthly statement.

- If you're behind at the moment, stop using your credit card.

- On large items wait 24 hours before purchasing.

- Use only one credit card for all expenses. Stay within your line of credit. Use this card for emergencies, for car rentals, hotel reservations, plane fare reservations, etc., when traveling to minimize the risks of carrying cash, and as a proof-of-purchase records, expense accounts, IRS receipts of purchases.

- If you have difficulty in properly using your credit card, freeze your card in a container in your freezer. You can't purchase until the ice thaws.

- Cut up your cards if you can't manage them.

- If you make a mistake while writing a check, correct it neatly and initial it. Write in permanent ink—don't use pencil or erasable pen.

PRAYER: Father God, I appreciate that You inspired men to talk
            about good financial planning in Your Word. May
            I have the wisdom to include them in my financial
            planning. Amen.

ACTION: Take one of these secrets for the next week and put it
            into practice. Do this for the next four weeks.

REFLECTIONS

Plow a Straight Row

Let your eyes look directly ahead, and let your
gaze be fixed straight in front of you.
PROVERBS 4:25

As a young boy when I went to my PaPa's farm in Texas during the summer time, he would take me along to the fields to plow his land. He had a team of donkeys and a draft horse to pull the multi-furrow plow. I can remember him telling me that in order to plow a straight row you have to keep your eyes on a distant object while you're plowing.

If you can plow a straight furrow or mow a lawn in a straight line by keeping your eyes fixed on a distant object, surely this principle should be true in everyday life—particularly if the object on which you fix your gaze is the same yesterday, today, and forever.

That's what Solomon, the writer of Proverbs, says in chapter 4. The complete book of Proverbs is about following a straight path. The book tells us...

- how to avoid the sexual trap (chapters 5–7).
- how to retain your integrity (12:1-16; 29:23).
- how to control your tongue (12:17-22; 21:23).
- how to get along with difficult people (14:7; 15:1).
- how to stay healthy and live long (3:7-8,13-18).

According to Solomon, the wise person can walk the straight path and not be misdirected.

A fool tells what he will do; a boaster tells what he has done; a wise man does it and says nothing.

—Unknown

The Bible tells us, "The fear of the Lord is the beginning of knowledge, but fools despise wisdom and discipline" (Proverbs 1:7). When Jesus was talking to Thomas, He said, "I am the way, and the truth, and the life; no one comes to the Father but through me" (John 14:6 nasb). So the only way to follow a straight path through life is to keep your eyes on Him.

———

PRAYER: Father God, let me focus on You, for wisdom begins by having the proper awe for who You are. My purpose in life is to know and enjoy You forever! Amen.

ACTION: The next time you mow your lawn look at an object in the distance and see how straight your row looks.

REFLECTIONS

Be Humble in Spirit

He has brought down rulers from their thrones,
and has exalted those who were humble.
LUKE 1:52 NASB

It's amazing in our culture today—the proud get exalted, and the humble get left behind. The old baseball saying "nice guys finish last" has come true in everyday life. The loudmouths in sports get the microphone to spout off, and the easygoing, quiet man sits by his locker and no one clamors for his interview.

> To learn humility is to learn contentment in all circumstances.
> Humility is not in what we own or achieve, but in maintaining a teachable attitude, a willingness to bend to the will of the Father.
>
> —JAN SILVIOUS

In the New Testament we find the word *humility* to mean a personal quality of dependence on God and respect for other people. It is not a natural human instinct, but it is a God-given virtue acquired through holy living.

While the mind of the natural man is selfish and proud, the essence of Jesus' mind is unselfish and loving toward others. Christ was our great example of a proper walk pleasing to God.

Our hearts must be transformed by the Holy Spirit so that we can reflect God's love to others through the humble example of Jesus.

Corrie ten Boom, an unbelievable Dutch woman who survived the horror of World War II while in the confines of the German death camps, received a lot of praise for what she did during her confinement, and yet she remained unfazed by all the tributes. When asked how she managed to stay so humble among all these honors, she humbly replied:

> I accept every compliment as a flower and say thank you, and each evening I put them in a bunch and lay them at Jesus' feet where the praise belongs.

Our world is full of men and women who are eager to take God's honor and heap it on their own heads. But God has a way of humbling us. From my own experience in life I know that I need to come before His throne with open arms and humbly bow before Him, seeking whatever He has for me in my life. We all need to learn this lesson of humility in life, because God has promised that if we don't humble ourselves, He will do it for us.

When Christ entered into the Greek world, they hated the quality of humility, but Jesus entered as a humble Savior. He became obedient to God's will, which led to His death on the cross. Throughout Jesus' walk on this earth He taught people to be humble before God and man.

In today's passage we see that God will exalt those who are humble. Humility comes from God and results in the praise of God.

> Unless you humble yourself before God in the dust, and confess before Him your iniquities and sins, the gate of heaven, which is open only for sinners saved by grace, must be shut against you forever.
>
> —DWIGHT L. MOODY

—✲—

PRAYER: Father God, may I continually look to Jesus to see the kind of man I want to be. May I take pride off the throne and put You up there. Amen.

ACTION: Lay your bunch of flowers at the foot of the cross today.

REFLECTIONS

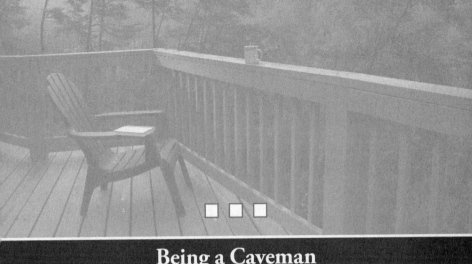

Being a Caveman

Give heed to my cry, for I am brought very low; deliver me from my persecutors, for they are too strong for me.

PSALM 142:6 NASB

Emilie and I were visiting the home of some new friends for the first time. Of course, we had to take a tour of their lovely home. The man of the family stayed ten feet back from the rest of us while his wife conducted the 50-cent tour, but as we got closer to the entertainment center, he nudged his way to the front of the tour. He wanted to make sure that everyone got a good view of his "man cave." He was so proud of his remodel. He had a big 52" high definition TV with surround speakers, six big overstuffed chaise lounge leather chairs with ottomans attached. He shared his delight as if he were a primitive caveman of prehistoric times.

In Psalm 142, David was stuck in a cave, but it was a different kind of cave from the one belonging to my gentleman friend. Some Bible scholars state that this was when David was running from King Saul, who wanted to kill him.

> David departed from there and escaped to the cave of Adullam;
> and when his brothers and all his father's household heard of it,
> they went down there to him.
>
> —1 SAMUEL 22:1 NASB

David was hounded by trouble and troublemakers. He was surrounded by those who wanted to take his life. Sensing he was surrounded and hemmed in by his foes, he decided to turn to God for help. Read Psalm 142.

193

- David was scared—he shared his thoughts with God (verse 2).

- He felt all by himself and that no one cared about him (verses 4-5).

- He was in a bad situation so he pleaded to God for his rescue (verse 6).

- David was trapped, so he pleaded for freedom (verse 7).

Our cave might not surround us like David's, but we men all have caves that surround us today. What does our cave look like (not our entertainment cave)? We might have despair brought on by sadness through a death, an illness, a failed marriage, a business that is coming apart. We might be caught in a cave brought on by poor decisions on our part, or maybe we have doubts about our lack of faith that has caused us to lose all joy and confidence in our Lord.

What did David do when he was trapped in his cave?

- He asked God for mercy.

- He sought refuge in God.

- He promised to use his freedom as a way to praise God.

Through all of his doubts his complaints were followed by faith; his desperation was followed by praise, and his aloneness was followed by fellowship. There is a lot to be learned by David, the caveman.

> The beginning of anxiety is the end of faith, and the beginning
> of true faith is the end of anxiety.
>
> —GEORGE MÜLLER

———∿∿∿———

PRAYER: Father God, let me learn from David so I won't have to be cooped-up in a dark, damp cave. Let me always stay transparent with Your righteousness. Amen.

ACTION: Think through this question, "What is your cave and what are you hiding from?"

REFLECTIONS

The Coming and Going of a Friend

A faithful friend is a strong defense: and he that
hath found such an one hath found a treasure.
ECCLESIASTICUS 6:14 (APOCRYPHA)

Today I find my heart heavy with sadness because Emilie and I have said goodbye to a dear couple that are relocating to a different part of the country. We have only known them for three years but over that time period we have come to know them as family. They were new in our community; we got them involved in our church and our small group Bible study that met in our home every Thursday night.

Some people you meet and you casually get to know, but there are others that just seem to bond as a brother. This couple was that kind of friend— Emilie liked her, and I liked him.

We are very excited for them and their future, but yet there is an emptiness in my heart today.

Emilie and I are who we are today because of all the various people who have touched our lives. We have been especially touched by this couple. Even though our hearts are saddened we rejoice that we touched each other's lives. None of us will ever be the same.

Maybe you as an individual or as a couple have these kinds of friendships. They may be friends from high school or friends you just recently met, but however long you have known them, they have had a mighty impact upon your life. Just appreciate that you have been their friend. Reach out and touch them with a smile, a hug, a meal together, a prayer together or just sitting on a bench looking out to the breaking waves on the beach.

You will never be the same because they came into your life just for a time in history.

> God evidently does not intend us all to be rich, or powerful, or great, but He does intend us all to be friends.
>
> —RALPH WALDO EMERSON

PRAYER: Father God, thank You for friends who touch my life—for a long or short period of time. They help make me who I am. Amen.

ACTION: Contact by mail, phone, or text message a friend and express to them how much they mean to you!

REFLECTIONS

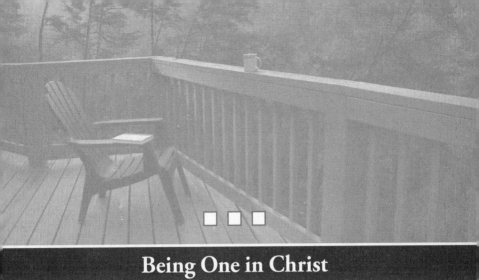

Being One in Christ

There is no partiality with God.
ROMANS 2:11 NASB

Quite often in a family the children will ask Mom and Dad which child they love the most. For some reason they sense a partiality and would like to know for themselves who is the favorite. As parents, we have to be alert to this feeling and make sure there is no partiality not only among our children but also in other relationships. In the book of James we read:

> My brethren, do not hold your faith in our glorious Lord Jesus Christ with an attitude of personal favoritism...but if you show partiality, you are committing sin and are convicted by the law as transgressors.
>
> —JAMES 2:1,9

Take a look at this story:

> A Sunday school superintendent was registering two new boys in Sunday school. She asked their ages and birthdays so she could place them in the appropriate classes. The bolder of the two replied, "We're both seven. My birthday is April 8 and my brother's birthday is April 20." The superintendent replied, "But that's not possible, boys." The quieter brother spoke up. "No, it's true. One of us is adopted."
>
> "Oh?" asked the superintendent, not convinced. "Which one?"

The two brothers looked at each other and smiled. The bolder one said, "We asked Dad that same question awhile ago, but he just looked at us and said he loved us both equally, and he couldn't remember anymore which one of us was adopted."[16]

As adopted sons of God, we fully share in the inheritance of His only begotten Son, Jesus. If Jesus can love us equally, then we can surely give to our children, friends, and new acquaintances no partiality regarding blessings or privileges.

—⁓—

PRAYER: Father God, You are our example in raising our children. As believers, each of us has equal inheritances of blessing and privileges. Help me to do the same for our children. Amen.

ACTION: How are you doing in this area of no partiality? What changes could be made?

REFLECTIONS

Living Life with Purpose

Even when we were with you, we used to give you this order:
if anyone will not work, then he is not to eat, either.
2 THESSALONIANS 3:10 NASB

We live in a world where some politicians want to provide food and housing to those who don't want to work—they just enjoy having the citizens pay for their upkeep. Then there are others who believe what Scripture teaches—no work, no pay. This is the dilemma that we face in America. Which way are we going to go? That's the big 64-dollar question.

Life can be boring or exciting, depending on which you choose. Take time to look at your life's purpose, and you can soon figure out how life is going. I've found that men who take the time to write out their "mission goals" and look to the future seem to have excitement for life, but those who have never thought out what life is all about and only live for the moment seem to be bored with life.

My suggestion for living a happy life is to live life with a purpose. Give yourself away with a cause. If you are interested in finding out how to learn about developing a "mission goal" for yourself, read *500 Plus Handy Hints for Every Husband,* published by Harvest House. I devote several chapters on how you can plan out your life with purpose. Andrew Murray said it so well:

> I have learned to place myself before God every day as a vessel
> to be filled with His Holy Spirit. He has given me the blessed

assurance that He, as the everlasting God, has guaranteed His own work in me.

Some of us are called to labor by plowing or planting or harvesting. But each of us has a special calling to be used as a worker for God.

Men often ask me, "Do you ever get tired of what you're doing?" To be honest with them, I say, "Yes, I do get tired of airports, security checks, delayed times, cancelled flights, different times zones, the demands of people, the many hours of research and writing of a book, but seldom do I get tired of the ministry of my work."

May you grasp the excitement of living life with a purpose. Do what you like to do before the Lord, and do it with all the energy and creativity you have, regardless of the social ranking or the prestige of the calling.

David the psalmist wrote in Psalm 37:4-5:

> Delight yourself in the LORD, and He will give you the desires of your heart. Commit your way to the LORD; trust also in Him, and He will do it (NASB).

Two words stand out to me in this passage: *delight* and *commit*. These are both action words that require us to do thinking and planning. Remember to live life with a purpose, not by accident. You can take control of your own life, so don't wait for others to determine your fate in life.

———

PRAYER: Father God, You know how exciting life is for me. I have so many wonderful things to accomplish. Give me the strength and health to encourage men to be all You have for them. Amen.

ACTION: In your journal write a mission statement expressing what you want out of life.

REFLECTIONS

Are You a Tare or Wheat?

*When the wheat sprouted and formed
heads, then the weeds also appeared.*
MATTHEW 13:26 NASB

A lady at our local bank told me a story recently that when they are trained at how to identify counterfeit currency, they have to study the real money so well that when they see a fake they can spot it quickly. Not that they know what the counterfeit looks and feels like, but that they know the real item. That's the way we are to be with our Christian faith. We know the real thing, so when we see the fake we know it's not from God.

In Matthew 13:24-26 Jesus tells a parable in which he contrasted tares with wheat—righteous individuals who will inherit the kingdom of heaven.

It's very difficult to tell the difference between the two when they are both young sprouts. It's not until they mature can you readily tell the difference. Only by their fruit can you really tell them apart.

As men, we must ask ourselves a very personal question: "Are we wheat or tares?" What does the fruit of my life tell about me?

Am I just going through the motions with my faith, or do I see fruit ripen in my walk with God? Can I see changes in my life, my wife's life, and my children's lives? Do I really make a difference in this world?

Do you know Jesus well enough that when something appears on TV or the Internet, you can tell it's in error? Do you suck in what everyone tells you, or are you able to say that's a fake?

Just because one is a regular churchgoer doesn't mean he is a wheat. In fact, many are tares in disguise. God knows who are His. His Spirit will not only bear witness with your spirit, but He has also given you the short epistle of 1 John so that you might inspect your own fruit and see if it gives evidence of one's true salvation.

Come face-to-face with this question, are you a wheat or a tare?

> All mankind is divided into three classes: those that are immovable, those that are movable, and those that move.
>
> —BEN FRANKLIN

—⤳⤳—

PRAYER: Father God, let my spirit be able to identify the differences between a wheat and a tare. May my life reflect the fruit of wheat. Amen.

ACTION: Decide today what your fruit will be for your life— move on that decision.

REFLECTIONS

Have the Right Perspective

*You are my refuge and my shield; I have
put my hope in your word.*
PSALM 119:114

People have asked me how I can be so upbeat when so many things around me are negative. I guess it's because of my perspective on life. Through Scripture and life experiences, I have come to trust that God has a master plan for my life. He knew me from the beginning of time. He knows my beginning, and He knows the end. He is the Alpha and the Omega. I've learned that He has taken care of me in the past, He is taking care of me in the present, thus I have assurance that He will take care of my future. A long time ago, I told God, "Thy will be done in my life."

His words give me so much comfort. I have learned that I can count on His promise. When the psalmist tells me that God is my shield and that His promises are my only source of hope, I believe it. God's character is one of honor, trust, and reliability that I can bank on for my well-being.

God's Word brings me light on a foggy day, it brings me hope when I become discouraged, and it helps me not to make a mountain out of a molehill. His Word gives me the right perspective on life. I know my time on earth is such a short time and my time with Him after this earthly experience will be for eternity.

Teach us to number our days aright, that we may gain a heart
of wisdom.

—PSALM 90:12

—◦◦◦—

PRAYER: Father God, thanks for sharing with me Your wisdom, so that I have hope for the future. Your Word gives me hope for that future. Where others fret and worry, You have given me an eternal perspective.

ACTION: Search Scripture to find a promise that you can put your faith in. Claim it as your theme verse for life.

REFLECTIONS

Take One Step at a Time

How do you know what is going to happen tomorrow? For the length of your lives is uncertain as the morning fog—now you see it; soon it is gone.
JAMES 4:15 TLB

Sometimes the hardest part of starting a new day is taking the first step. Unfortunately, we all seem to pack too much in a 24-hour period. Good time management warns against that, because we soon get behind, and we spend the rest of the day trying to catch up. A good example is making a dental or doctor's appointment. Regardless what time I make the appointment, I have to wait one hour in the reception area.

In an old McGuffey Reader, I found a story about a clock that had been running for a long, long time on a mantelpiece. One day, the clock began to think about how many times during the year ahead it would have to tick. It counted up the seconds—31,536,000 in one year. The old clock just got too tired and thought, "I can't do it." It stopped right there. When somebody reminded the clock that it didn't have to tick the 31,536,000 seconds all at one time—but rather one by one—it began to run again, and everything was all right.

> Young people, it's wonderful to be young! Enjoy every minute of it. Do everything you want to do; take it all in. But remember that you must give an account to God for everything you do.
>
> —ECCLESIASTES 11:9 NLT

Sometimes when I get out of bed early in the morning, the day ahead of me looks very long. So many things to do—appointments to keep, a yearly chest x-ray, meeting with my CPA regularly regarding some tax questions, a lunch with my support group. Many days can be 10 to 12 hours long.

To be honest, sometimes I want to forget it all and crawl back into bed for another hour or two. But a small voice inside of me says, "Bob, you don't have to do it all at once. Just put your feet on the floor and take the first step of the day." Break up the large block of the day into little pieces. A long journey begins with the first step.

Hard work means prosperity; only a fool idles away his time.

—PROVERBS 12:11 TLB

PRAYER: Father God, thank You for allowing me to see the whole picture and for helping me realize it doesn't have to be accomplished all at once. Amen.

ACTION: Just put your feet on the floor—then begin your journey.

REFLECTIONS

Celebrate Each Day

If only they were wise and would understand
this and discern what their end will be!
DEUTERONOMY 32:29

How often do we talk in terms of days? Usually our reference is in terms of years. She's 37 years old, they were married 15 years ago, I've been sober for 10 years. World War II was 68 years ago.

One thing about youth is that they think they have nine lives and they will never get old. They think they are "eternally young," but as we get older, we realize that we are running out of years, and our thoughts turn to months and to days.

Today's verse suggests that we are to number our days. We are encouraged to live each day to the fullest so that when our lives draw to an end, we have gained a "heart of wisdom" or have spent each day as we should. When we live each day unto the Lord, we live it with gusto and enthusiasm for Him.

I have found that as I get older, the inevitables of life happen, and I must learn to adjust to the unknowns that appear from time to time. One cannot do this in terms of years but only from day-to-day and often from hour-to-hour. Aging isn't a choice—it just happens, and it isn't always the "golden years"—they don't have as much gold as we thought.

With each new pain and ache, don't become negative, but rather celebrate the life that God has given you. How we respond to these aches will determine how we grow old.

—✳—

PRAYER: Father God, let me enjoy each day as if it were my last day. Let my eyes see Your beauty of nature and my nose smell the fragrance of Your flower. Each day is all I have. Amen.

ACTION: Do what you would do if you only had one day to live. Share it with a friend.

REFLECTIONS

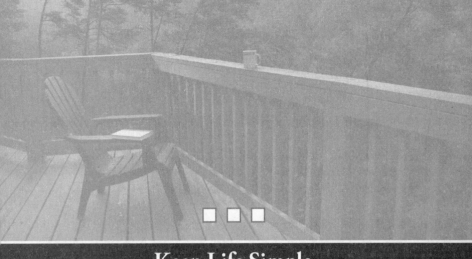

Keep Life Simple

But I am afraid that just as Eve was deceived by the serpent's cunning, your minds may somehow be led astray from your sincere and pure devotion to Christ.

2 Corinthians 11:3

As we look at our society today we have such a cross-section of so many things:

- How we dress.
- What are our standards.
- Who determines what is right and wrong.
- What is moral or immoral.
- How to act.

Who sets these standards, where do they come from, and what is their beginning? Just sit in front of your television for a couple of hours and listen with a discerning ear to what's being said and what's being shown. Jot down what's being said and what you hear. With each entry, compare the deviation from God's standard. What are the differences?

Then look in the mirror and see where you want to be in the differences. Do you want God's standard or the media's standard? After all, you the consumer must make the final choice. Do you want to imitate what you read about, the words to the music you listen to, or the body camouflage you see on the rock stars or the prison inmates?

Where are you in the world? Who sets your standards for today's culture war? Are you closer to God's standard or the culture's? How does that make you feel?

> Somewhere along the line of our development we discover what we really are, and then we make our decision for which we are responsible. Make that decision primarily for yourself because you can never live anyone else's life.
>
> —ELEANOR ROOSEVELT

Emilie and I recently had a friend tell us that we have a very sheltered life. At first, I was taken aback, but after some thought, I said, "It is by our choice, and thank you—that's a real compliment." In life, it's often not good to be called "cool." We like the simple and pure life given by living close to Jesus.

Is there any danger that possibly we've been "led astray from the simplicity and purity of devotion to Christ" (NASB)? As you continue to look into that mirror, what do you see reflecting back to you? Whose friend are you?

> In every success story, you find someone has made a courageous decision.
>
> —PETER DRUCKER

—◦◦◦—

PRAYER: Father God, give me the courage to resist all the media hype that tries to tell me who I am and what I should look like. Amen.

ACTION: What changes need to be made in your life to be more like Jesus? Jot them down in your journal. Ask a friend to hold you accountable.

REFLECTIONS

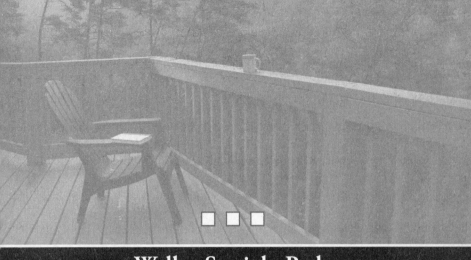

Walk a Straight Path

My foot has held fast to His path.
JOB 23:11 NASB

It amazes me how many of us walk a crooked path and expect it to be straight. In computer language, we hear the famous term, "Junk in, junk out." If we live a carefree life, we will have a carefree ending. I'm always reading obituaries, and I often read one about a young person who had been killed in an accident. Many times, it characterizes the person as one who liked to live life to the fullest and seemed to always test the boundaries. In simple terms that translates into, "Here's a person who lived a crooked path."

It's hard to sit back and watch a person make bad choices in life. How do people manage to so quickly mess up their lives? I believe it's because they have not valued God's Word enough. They invest more in temporal things than eternal values. We don't take time out of our busy lives to know His Word in such a way that it becomes a light to our feet and a lamp to our paths. Where there is no light, we have darkness, and in darkness we will stumble.

God's servant Job understood that the only way to walk safely through the trials, tragedies, and testing of this life is to set our feet firmly in the way of truth:

- My foot has held fast to His path;
- I have kept His way and not turned aside.
- I have not departed from the command of His lips;

213

- I have treasured the words of His mouth more than my necessary food.

—JOB 23:11-12 NASB

In one of our recent home Bible studies, a young lady came up to me after the study and remarked, "I didn't know that was in the Bible!" Devoted time in God's Word is vital if you're going to have a pure heart.

Paul in Romans 12:2 shows us our two struggles in life. We either conform to the world or we are transformed by the renewing of our minds. So many of us have conformed to the world instead of being transformed. That's why lives, homes, and relationships are in such tragic conditions.

Walking a crooked path is much more fatiguing than walking a well-lit straight path. When you end up at your final destination, you will have saved yourself a lot of worry and stress. The Holy Spirit gives you a peace that lights up the dark corners of your life. Get to know God's Word and what it says. After a short period of time you will find that the Lord will begin to straighten out your crooked path.

—◦◦◦—

PRAYER: Father God, may I fall in love with Your Word—give me the desire to spend time with You each day. I want You to light up my path. Amen.

ACTION: Select one thing in your life that you want to straighten out. List in your journal two or three things that you plan to incorporate to make this change.

REFLECTIONS

A Look at Anger

Good sense makes a man restrain his anger, and it is
his glory to overlook a transgression or an offence.
PROVERBS 19:11 AMP

A nger burns like a hot brushfire. As I read my daily newspaper and view
the TV news, I am constantly reminded of the sin of anger. Not a
day goes by when the media doesn't report the sad results of anger: murder,
road rage, drunk driving, drive-by assaults, arson fires, child beating, rape,
and so on.

A healthy relationship cannot exist where anger exists. The two do not
go together. In order for healthy relationships and friendships to flourish,
we must be able to control this raging fire that exists in us. The book of
Proverbs gives some insight concerning the subject of anger.

These passages are from The Living Bible:

- "A short-tempered man is a fool. He hates the man who is
  patient" (14:17).

- "A quick-tempered man starts fights; a cool-tempered man
  tries to stop them" (15:18).

- "It is better to be slow-tempered than famous; it is better to
  have self-control than to control an army" (16:32).

- "A fool gets into constant fights. His mouth is his undoing!
  His words endanger him" (18:6-7).

- "A short-tempered man must bear his own penalty; you can't do much to help him. If you try once you must try a dozen times!" (19:19).

- "Keep away from angry, short-tempered men, lest you learn to be like them and endanger your soul" (22:24-25).

- "A rebel shouts in anger; a wise man holds his temper in and cools it" (29:11).

- "There is more hope for a fool than for a man of quick temper" (29:20).

- "A hot-tempered man starts fights and gets into all kinds of trouble" (29:22).

If anger is one of your enemies, go to God in prayer and ask for healing. Anger is a cancer that can destroy your body if not addressed. Don't wait until it is too late. Healthy relationships demand that anger be conquered.

———

PRAYER: Father God, help me examine myself to see if there is any evidence of anger in my life. If so, I want to give it to You. Amen.

ACTION: Examine yourself to see if there is any anger in your soul.

REFLECTIONS

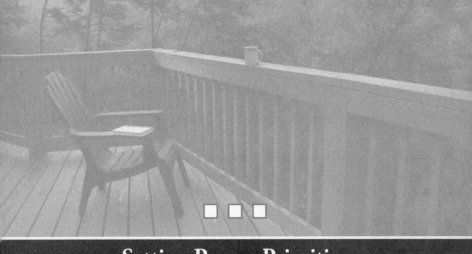

Setting Proper Priorities

*Husbands, love your wives, just as Christ also loved
the church and gave Himself up for her.*
EPHESIANS 5:25 NASB

Men, we are all busy. There are many forces pulling us away from the priorities we have as husbands. Satan would love to make us so busy that we neglect our wives and children.

A well-known preacher, W.E. Sangster, announced to his wife early in their marriage, "I can't be a good husband and a good minister. I am going to be a good minister."

Pastor Sangster had a very demanding schedule not only in his own church, but he was asked to speak all over the world. When he was at home, he seldom gave any attention to his wife and children. He did not help with any of the household chores. He was there in body, but certainly not in spirit. He had forgotten to put into practice God's first commandment regarding marriage.

> A man shall leave his father and his mother, and shall cleave to
> his wife: and they shall become one flesh.
>
> —GENESIS 2:24 KJV

Reverend Sangster probably did love his wife, but he had lost sight of what came first—his ministry or his wife and children. He could have been a better husband and a better minister if he had been more concerned for their needs than his busy schedule.

Many of us have many demands on our time—some of them are unavoidable. But if we as Christian husbands and fathers take seriously the instruction of Paul, we will love our wives as Jesus loved His church. In fact, Christ died on the cross for the church. Many of us would say we would die for our wives. Then why don't we live for them?

Someday we will stand before God and He will ask us one question, "Is your wife a better Christian because she was married to you?" How will you answer Him?

> The woman was not taken
> From Adam's head, we know,
> To show she must not rule him—
> 'Tis evidently so.
> The woman she was taken
> From under Adam's arm,
> So she must be protected
> From injuries and harm.
>
> —Abraham Lincoln

Prayer: Father God, don't let my busy schedule prevent me from spending quality time with my wife and family. Amen.

Action: Evaluate the importance you place on your wife. If you're not happy with it—make a few changes.

Reflections

Trust and Obey

Do not worry about tomorrow.
MATTHEW 6:34

Do you know that statistically 85 percent of the things we worry about never happen? Americans have become a nation of worriers—we worry about everything, our mortgage payment, our wives, our children, our economy, our finances. On and on, we always seem to have a cause to worry about.

Just what kind of Father do you think we have? Is He faithless or faithful? Can He tell a lie?

Of course not. He can never lie. What He says we can believe. He is always faithful. Paul wrote to Timothy in 2 Timothy 2:13, "If we are faithless, he remains faithful, for He cannot disown Himself."

You can surely trust Him, so stop being so anxious. It's so unnecessary! When we question His faithfulness, we are really questioning God.

Jesus reassures us by His words in Matthew 6:26:

> Look at the birds of the air; they do not sow or reap or store away in barns, and yet your heavenly Father feeds them. Are you not much more valuable than they?

We are to live one day at a time. That's why Jesus taught us to pray, "Give us each day our daily bread" (Luke 11:3). If He took care of you yesterday and today, He will surely take care of you tomorrow.

PRAYER: Father God, let me turn my anxiousness over to You. Help me realize that 85 percent of my worries are useless. I want to look to You for my guidance. Amen.

ACTION: List in your journal five worries that you are going to turn over to God.

REFLECTIONS

How to Teach Your Children About Money

Let no debt remain outstanding, except the continuing debt to love one another, for he who loves his fellowman has fulfilled the law.
ROMANS 13:8

We live in a world where adults often find themselves in financial woes. Where do we learn about money? Usually by trial and error, since few families take the time to teach their children how to be smart with money. Yet, at an early age, children should know about money and what it can do for them.

Children who learn about money at an early age will be ahead in this mystery game. Learning to deal with money properly will foster discipline, good work habits, and self-respect.

Here are eight ways in which you can help your children get a good handle on money:

1. *Start with an allowance.* Most experts advise that an allowance should not be tied directly to a child's daily chores. Children should help around the home not because they get paid for it but because they share responsibilities as members of a family. However, you might pay a child for doing extra jobs at home. An allowance is a vital tool for teaching children how to budget, save, and make their own decisions. Children learn from their mistakes when their own money has been lost or spent foolishly.

2. *Model the proper use of credit.* Explain to your children the conditions of when it's necessary to use credit and the importance of paying their loan back on a timely basis. You can make this a great teaching tool. Give them practice in filling out credit forms. Their first loan might be from you to them for a special purpose.

3. *Teach your children how to save.* One of the first ways to begin teaching the concept of saving is to give them some form of a piggy bank. Spare change or extra earnings can go into the piggy bank. When it gets full, you might want to open an account at your local bank. When your children are older, you might want to establish a passbook account at a local bank so they can go to the bank and personally deposit money in their account. Children who learn how to save will better appreciate what they've worked to acquire.

4. *Show them how to be wise in their spending.* Take your children with you when you shop, and show them some cost comparisons. They will soon see that with little effort, they can save a lot of money. You might want to demonstrate this principle to them in a tangible way when they want to purchase a larger item for themselves. Go with them to several stores to look for that one item, writing down the highest price. This way they can really see how much they can save by comparison shopping. In our high-tech society, feel free to surf the Internet. Most items can be found on the World Wide Web. Clothing is an area where a lot of lessons on wise spending can be made. After a while, your children will realize that designer clothes cost a lot more just for that particular label or patch.

5. *Let them work part-time.* There are many excellent part-time jobs waiting for your children. Fast-food outlets, markets, malls, nanny, babysitting, dog walking, etc., can give valuable work experience to your children. Some entrepreneurial youngsters even begin a thriving business based on their skills and interests. These part-time jobs are real confidence-boosters. Just help your child keep a proper balance between

work, home, church, and school. A limit of 10 to 15 hours per week might be a good guideline.

6. *Let them help you with your budgeting.* Encourage your children to help you budget for the family finances. This gives them experience in real-life money matters. They also get a better idea about your family's income and expenses. Children can often have good suggestions about how to better utilize the family finances, and their experience can give them a better understanding of why your family can't afford certain wants. Give them experience in writing out the checks (of course, Mom or Dad will have to sign them), balancing the checkbook, and making deposits at the bank. All of these experiences are very valuable for future skills in money management.

7. *Give them experience in handling adult expenses.* As your children get older, they need to experience real-life costs. Since children normally live at home, they don't always understand true-to-life expenses. Let them experience paying for their own telephone (cell phone), car expenses, and clothing expenses (the ones with the labels and badges). Depending upon their age and job income, have them pay a portion of the utility and household bills. This can be an eye-opener for them, and it could become a valuable experience for children who have left school and/or still live at home. (This will also motivate them to want to leave home and to live on their own—this helps cut the cord and motivates them to become more independent.)

8. *Show them how to give to the Lord.* At a very young stage in life, parents and children should talk about where things come from. The children should be aware that all things are given from God and that He is just letting us borrow them for a short time on earth. Children can understand that we are to return back to God what He has so abundantly given to us. This principle can be experienced through Sunday school or their church offering. When special projects at church come up, you might want to review these needs with

your children so they can decide whether they want to give extra money above what they normally give to their church. Learning to give their time as a volunteer, such as serving Thanksgiving meals to the homeless, offer invaluable lessons in having a servant's heart.

Woe to him who increases what is not his...will not your creditors rise up suddenly...indeed you will become plunder for them.

—Habakkuk 2:6-7 nasb

—◠◠◠—

Prayer: Father God, let my use of money be a positive example to my children. May they catch on how to manage money properly while they are young. Amen.

Action: If you haven't already started, begin today to share your good skills with your children. It doesn't start until you start. Remember, precept upon precept.

Reflections

A Ship in the Night

You will know the truth, and the truth will set you free.
John 8:32

The book of Proverbs stresses the importance of three big words:

- Wisdom
- Knowledge
- Understanding

We live in a day where individuals want to do their thing. They feel that no one can give as good counsel as themselves. Isn't it difficult to change when you think you are right? We get so stubborn that we won't change our thoughts and opinions for anything. "Why should I? I'm right!" we say.

One foggy night the captain of a large ship saw another ship's lights approaching. This other ship was on a course that would mean a head-on crash. Quickly the captain signaled to the approaching ship, "Please change your course 10 degrees west." The reply came blinking back through the thick fog, "You change your course 10 degrees east."

Indignantly the captain pulled rank and shot a message back to the other ship, "I'm a sea captain with 35 years of experience. You change your course 10 degrees west!" Without hesitation the signal flashed back, "I'm a seaman fourth-class. You change your course 10 degrees east!"

Enraged, the captain realized that within minutes they would crash head-on, so he blazed his final warning: "I'm a 50,000-ton freighter. Change your course!" The simple message winked back, "I'm a lighthouse. You change..."[17]

You, too, may get so frustrated with your mate that you give out stern warnings that the other person must change course. Because of past experiences, they may not want to budge from their respective positions. Satan would love to destroy your relationship using the differences in the way you like to do things. I petition both of you today to be set free from stubbornness.

In Ephesians 5:21 we read, "Be subject to one another in the fear of Christ."

With this attitude you are free to serve others. Anything less than this allows selfishness and pride to enter into your life, creating an unwillingness to change.

Be willing to alter your course rather than insisting on your own way.

> Pay attention and learn good judgment, for I am giving you good guidance. Don't turn away from my teaching.
>
> —PROVERBS 4:1-2 NLT

—⟳—

PRAYER: Father God, let us always remain flexible. We don't want to break apart when we move. Amen.

ACTION: Think of one thing in your relationship that needs to be changed. You be willing to make the change.

REFLECTIONS

No Little White Lies

*Join with others in following my example, brothers, and take
note of those who live accordingly to the pattern we gave you.*
PHILIPPIANS 3:17

The big motto for this year is, "Be a man of integrity." In other words, are you a man I can trust? We have a new president who will determine the future of our country. Our country is still polarized, though, and politicians on both sides of the aisle are trying to convince the American public that they have more character and integrity than their political opponents.

We should ask each of them (including our new president), "Will your words and actions today reveal you to others as a man of honesty and integrity? Is your walk honest before God? Can others trust you...or do you cheat?" As individual men, we may not be better qualified than our new president, but God is asking us the same question. Is our walk the same as our talk? We knew of a very successful businessman from our past church that thought he was a good Christian whenever he was in church, but what he did out of church was different. He no longer felt that he needed to live out Christian values in his business dealings. Consequently he did not have a good reputation in the local community. He was not known as a man you could trust—he had little integrity.

Cheating can take all sorts of forms. It doesn't necessarily have to be when taking an exam in school. There are many ways to cheat—you can give false witness, you can fudge on your tax return, you cannot follow through on what you verbally or contractually said, you can exaggerate, you can falsify your business expense. You can tell a lot of "little white lies."

Job determined not to lower his standards or to buy into the justification that, "Everyone else is doing it, why can't I?"

> Till I die, I will not deny my integrity.
>
> —Job 27:5

Can I say the same? What's my contribution to the moral fiber of our country? I want to say what Paul said in the midst of a corrupt Roman Empire, "Be imitators of me, just as I also am of Christ" (1 Corinthians 11:1 nasb).

> Fire tests the purity of silver and gold, but a person is tested by being praised.
>
> —Proverbs 27:21

———

Prayer: Father God, I want to be known as a 24/7 Christian. I look into Your mirror each day (the Bible) to check on my walk versus my talk. Your Word helps me to stay on a straight path. Amen.

Action: Ask a very close friend to see if he thinks your talk and walk are together.

REFLECTIONS

Man's Moon Walk

*The Word [Jesus] became flesh
and made his dwelling among us.*
JOHN 1:14

I was a young man when Apollo 15 had a historic moon walk. The world's TV audience was anxiously glued to their TV sets observing this landing. Colonel James Irwin, upon coming back to earth, related some of the highpoints of his experience. He told of the crew's weightless bodies floating free in the space capsule, the rising crescent of the earth as seen from the moon, and the victorious splashdown reentering our atmosphere.

He also spoke of the impact the experience had on his spiritual life. He said that from the lunar surface he sensed both the awe of God and the struggle of earthbound man and woman. As he came back to earth he realized he couldn't be content with just being someone special—he wanted to tell others how to live a better life. In his speeches he concluded by saying that if we think it is a great event to go to the moon, how much greater is the wonder that God came to earth in the person of our Savior, Jesus Christ.

Through this breakthrough in our space program, science and technology have made great advances. But to decide the more important event between man walking on the moon or God walking on the earth, I choose the latter event. Because God joined man on earth we are able to know both our origin and destiny. We can know the joy of having our sins forgiven and can know the abundant life (John 10:10) that He wants us to have.

I used to ask God to help me. Then I asked if I might help Him. I ended up by asking Him to do His work through me.

—HUDSON TAYLOR

⁓

PRAYER: Father God, may I always be in awe when I think what man has done in my life, but may I be in double awe when I think of what You have done for man. Amen.

ACTION: Be reminded again that God sent His Son, Jesus, to come to earth to save man from his sins.

REFLECTIONS

Put on the New

Choose life in order that you may live,
you and your descendants.
DEUTERONOMY 30:19 NASB

Life is a strange journey. We have two choices to make. We choose either life or death. It's that basic. Not too much mental power is needed to figure this formula out.

> If anyone is in Christ, he is a new creation; the old has gone, the new has come!
>
> —2 CORINTHIANS 5:17

What are those old things? They are the natural things that men are born with. Those things that we need to flee from:

> Put to death the sinful, earthly things lurking within you. Have nothing to do with sexual immorality, impurity, lust, and evil desires. Don't be greedy, for a greedy person is an idolater, worshipping the things of this world. Because of these sins, the anger of God is coming. You used to do these things when your life was still part of this world. But now is the time to get rid of anger, rage, malicious behavior, slander, and dirty language. Don't lie to each other, for you have stripped off your old sinful nature and all its wicked deeds.
>
> —COLOSSIANS 3:5-9 NLT

These are the things we need to put off:

- anger
- rage
- malicious behavior
- slander
- dirty language
- lying

You might ask yourself, "Boy, do I have to give up all of these?" "What harm is there in keeping a few?" When you choose to keep any one of these, in essence you are choosing death. We must come clean and realize that these will eventually pull us away from God. He has a plan that spells out life and His perfect will for our lives is that we run as fast as we can from these death items. It means we will be choosing new friends, telling different jokes, reading different magazines, holding our tongue when we want to scream in anger. No more gossiping or using foul language. These are all death angels to relationships and particularly our marriage and family.

If not these, what must I put on? What does the new life look life?

> Put on your new nature, and be renewed as you learn to know your Creator and become like him. In this new life, it doesn't matter if you are Jew or Gentile, circumcised or uncircumcised, barbaric, uncivilized, slave, or free. Christ is all that matters, and he lives in all of us. Since God chose you to be holy people whom he loves, you must clothe yourselves with tenderhearted mercy, kindness, humility, gentleness, and patience. Make allowance for each other's faults, and forgive the person who offends you. Remember, the Lord forgave you, so you must forgive others. Above all, clothe yourselves with love, which binds us all together in perfect harmony.
>
> —COLOSSIANS 3:10-14 NLT

What do we need to put on?

- mercy
- kindness
- humility
- gentleness

- patience
- forgiveness
- love

We must be willing to take those things off that lead to death and to put on those things that give life.

———

PRAYER: Father God, give me the courage and strength to take off those things that will prevent me from being all You want me to be. I so want to be the man after Your own heart. Amen.

ACTION: Make a list of the things you want to put off. Save some room to list what you're going to do to put them off. Give yourself a deadline for accomplishing each. Then do the same for what you want to put on.

REFLECTIONS

Where Do I Find Happiness?

How blessed [happy] is the man who does not walk in the counsel of the wicked...but his delight is in the law of the Lord.
—Psalm 1:1-2 NASB

We seem to live in a world that wants to be happy. Wherever we turn we are bombarded by the media telling us how we can be happy. All the way from the car we drive, the clothes we wear, the restaurants we select, the homes we purchase. If only we had these things we would finally find happiness.

Eight men were once traveling together, and each related his experience in reply to the question "Are you fully happy?" A banker said he had acquired a fortune, which was invested securely; he had a lovely and devoted family, yet the thought that he must leave them all forever cast a funeral pall over the declining years of his life.

A military officer said he had known glory and the intoxication of triumph; but after the battle he passed over the field and found a brother officer dying. He tried to relieve him, but the dying man said, "Thank you, but it's too late. We must all die; think about it, think about it." This scene gripped the officer, and he could find no deliverance from it. So he confessed his unhappiness.

A diplomat spoke of the honors and gratitude showered upon

him during a long and successful career, yet confessed an emptiness of the heart, a secret malady which all his honors could not cure.

A poet told of the pleasures he enjoyed with the muses; of the applause of the people; of his fame, which he was assured was immortal. But, dissatisfied, he cried out, "What is such an immortality?" and declared his unsatisfied longing for a higher immortality.

A man of the world said that his effort had been to laugh at everything—to look at the bright side of things and be happy; to find pleasure in the ballroom, theater, and other amusements; yet he confessed that he was sometimes melancholy, and was far from perfectly happy.

A lawyer said he had health, wealth, reputation, and a good marriage, and that during his career he longed for just what he now possessed; but he did not find the expected enjoyment in it, and contentment was not his heritage. His hours were long and his existence monotonous; he was not fully happy.

A religious professor, a ritualist, professed his strict adherence to the doctrines of the gospel and his punctual performance of religious duties, without being happy at all.

A Christian physician related his vain search for happiness in the world and in his profession; but then he had been led by Scripture to see himself a sinner and to look to Christ as his Savior. Since that time he found peace, contentment, and joy, and had no fear of the end, which to him was only the beginning.[18]

One of man's quests for life is learning how to be happy. We try all kinds of things to make us happy, but after experiencing them we still aren't happy. At the end of each of these pursuits we are supposed to find this magic thing called happiness. But to our amazement, when we finally arrive at this great destination we often find that happiness has moved and left no forwarding address.

This tension is one of life's greatest struggles: How do we balance between things and happiness? Read the great lessons found in the book of Proverbs, it will help you gain the wisdom to pursue life and gain the most peace and happiness.

PRAYER: Father God, I too struggle with this balance between things and happiness. Let me continue to go to Your Word to find this delicate balance. Amen.

ACTION: Today, start reading the book of Proverbs.

REFLECTIONS

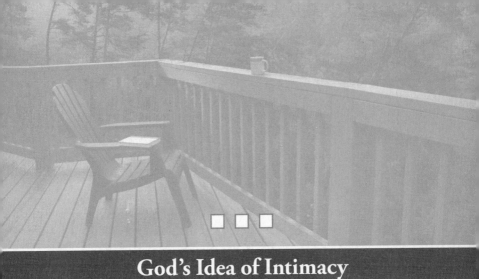

God's Idea of Intimacy

*A man shall leave his father and mother and be joined
to his wife, and they shall become one flesh.*

GENESIS 2:24 NKJV

The Bible's teaching on marriage has helped me learn about God's master plan for husbands and wives. One of the most important passages I have discovered is found in 1 Corinthians 7:1-5.

> It is good for a man not to touch a woman. But because of immoralities, let each man have his own wife, and each woman is to have her own husband. The husband must fulfill his duty to his wife, and likewise also the wife to her husband. The wife does not have authority over her own body, but the husband does; and likewise also the husband does not have authority over his own body, but the wife does. Stop depriving one another, except by agreement for a time that you may devote yourselves to prayer, and come together again so that Satan will not tempt you because of your lack of self-control (NASB).

These verses provide four solid guidelines for couples who desire love and intimacy in their relationship.

1. *Be faithful to one person.* God's Word clearly commands us to be faithful to one spouse (Exodus 20:14; Matthew 5:27-32; 19:18).

2. *Be available to each other.* A husband is to give of himself to fulfill his wife's needs, and the wife is to give of herself to fulfill her husband's needs. We are to freely ask for and give affection to one another.

3. *Submit to each other.* Be willing to submit to your mate in every way, meeting all her needs.

4. *Keep on meeting your mate's sexual needs.* Paul notes that the only exception to this guideline is taking time for prayer and fasting. Other than those specified times, a husband and wife should be available to each other and always seek to meet the other's needs.

Marriage is a sacred vow or commitment that you both made before God, and it is a very serious matter to break that vow. God gave marriage to us for our happiness, and I believe with his help you can discover what it means to build your lives together on Christ's foundation.

—BILLY GRAHAM

The Bible offers rich insight into the marriage relationship. I encourage you to spend some time studying what God's Word teaches about your marriage. Knowing and following the Creator's master plan will enrich your marriage—sexually and otherwise.

———

PRAYER: Father God, I want to have a godly intimacy with my wife. Let me see and understand the importance of having such a deep relationship with my woman. Clear my spirit to receive this teaching. Amen.

ACTION: Sit on the sofa this evening and hug your wife—nothing beyond a hug.

REFLECTIONS

Don't Forget

Beware, lest you forget the LORD your God by not keeping His commandments and His ordinances and His statutes which I am commanding you today.

Deuteronomy 8:11 NASB

One of the disadvantages of getting older is not being able to remember things as well as when you were younger. I've drawn embarrassing blanks on many things, such as telephone numbers, or when I've had to introduce a friend and I forget their name. I've walked to the refrigerator and can't recall why I'm there. I've even been embarrassed by going to the dishwasher when I intended to go to the trash compactor.

In Deuteronomy 8, Moses reminded the Israelites repeatedly that they were prone to forget God. He told them that when times got better they would forget what the Lord had done for them when times were bad. He wanted to caution them that the luxury of prosperity could make it easy to forget how dependent they were on the Lord at all times. They needed to realize that without the strength God provided they couldn't even raise their food to their mouths.

> God doesn't promise to take things from you, but He will be with you through your situation.
>
> —Kenton Beshore

Moses' instructions also apply to us. We must keep remembering what God has done for us, praising Him for what He has given us, and thanking

Him for His forgiveness. But above all, the Lord Himself is worth remembering just for who He is.

Make it a mental exercise to refresh in your mind all that God has done for you. How would life be different than it is now if you hadn't met Jesus along the way?

It's one thing to forget a person's name, but never forget what Jesus did for you and me on the cross.

> Count your blessings;
> Name them one by one.
> Count your many blessings;
> See what God hath done.
>
> —JOHNSON OATMAN, JR.

—◦◦◦—

PRAYER: Father God, may I never forget who You are and what You've done for me. The cross is always on my mind. Thank You! Amen.

ACTION: In your journal write down five blessings you never want to forget.

REFLECTIONS

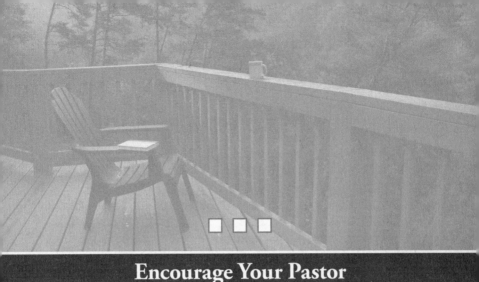

Encourage Your Pastor

Remember your leaders, who spoke the word of God to you.
HEBREWS 13:7

A pastor friend of ours recalls a large Promise Keepers gathering in Los Angeles where the master of ceremonies requested that all the pastors in the crowd come onto the stadium floor. As thousands of faithful pastors came forward, the remaining 60,000 men in the stadium stood up and started to clap, shout, and whistle. The roar of the men became deafening. The applause lasted for at least two minutes. Recognition for the pastors' faithfulness in ministry was long overdue. As the emcee finished giving honor to these servants of God, the audience again gave another standing ovation. Our friend said tears came down his cheeks as he heard such approval from those in attendance.

> He has honor if he holds himself to an ideal of conduct though
> it is inconvenient, unprofitable, or dangerous to do so.
>
> —WALTER LIPPMANN

Have you taken the time to encourage your pastor for their role in feeding the flock of God and overseeing their spiritual welfare? We often take for granted that week after week our minister will study and prepare a sermon that will reach us with God's truth. Often they feel unappreciated. Though they aren't looking for praise, they do need the encouragement of those who are helped by their dedication to your church.

———♦———

PRAYER: Father God, thank You for giving us a wonderful pastor who encourages our walk with You. Please bless his life and family today.

ACTION: Grab a cup of coffee and get to know your pastor better.

REFLECTIONS

Shout from the Housetop

We are not doing right. This day is a day of
good news, but we are keeping silent.
2 KINGS 7:9

O ne of the best forms of advertising is to tell someone about a good experience you have had with a doctor, an auto repair shop, or a new restaurant. Sharing helpful and encouraging information is something in which we usually find delight.

Many of us, though, are less eager to share the best news in all the world with others—that Christ can satisfy their spiritual hunger. There are some places in Scripture where Jesus tells us to share the "good news."

> Go therefore and make disciples of all the nations, baptizing them
> in the name of the Father and the Son and the Holy Spirit.
> —MATTHEW 28:19 NASB

> You shall be My witnesses both in Jerusalem, and in all Judea
> and Samaria, and even to the remotest part of the earth.
> —ACTS 1:8 NASB

God will hold us accountable for our obedience to Him when we stand before Him. In 2 Kings 7, we read where four starving lepers, in quarantine outside of Jerusalem, decided to surrender to the enemy soldiers who were overtaking the city in battle. But they found the Syrian camp empty of men and full of provisions, evidence of a terror-stricken flight. They ate to their fill and stashed away gold, silver, and clothing. But their feelings of guilt mixed with fear of being punished motivated them to share the good information with the hungry people of the city.

As believers let's not hold back the good news of what gives us hope for the future. We hold the key to unlocking the questions, "Why are we here on earth? What is our purpose?" Surely it's more than living day-to-day, going to work, coming home, having dinner, watching TV, going to sleep and starting the cycle all over tomorrow.

—⁓—

PRAYER: Father God, let me share with others what I've seen and heard—the Good News of Jesus. Give me a boldness to tell others. Amen.

ACTION: Share the Good News with someone today!

REFLECTIONS

Thirst for Water

Unless one is born of water and the Spirit,
he cannot enter in the kingdom of God.
JOHN 3:5 NASB

The big movement in the workout industry is to get people to drink more and more water. I work out at the gym three times a week and our instructor wants us to drink plenty of water. She recommends that you take your weight, divide by 2, and that's the number of ounces you need to drink daily. For example, if you weigh 200 pounds, you would need to drink 100 ounces of water daily. Drinking an adequate amount of water daily may reduce the risk of heart attack, give your skin a healthier look, and can even help you lose weight. On hot days and when we exercise we should consider drinking more ounces than we normally require. Even if we're not thirsty, we ought to drink water anyway.

The health experts tell us that if we wait until we are thirsty we've waited too long. Drink before your body tells you to drink. Dehydration sets in and you can get dizzy, tremble, and might even faint. Be extra cautious if you live in a hot weather zone.

Do you remember the time when you were thirsty for more of God? You couldn't read and study His Word often enough. Every page seemed to hold new promises and knowledge for you. When our walk is at its best, we want to be nearer and nearer to God.

Often when I'm out in the world and see the depravity of man, I have an increased desire to be close to the peace and comfort of the Scriptures.

Spiritual thirst is often used in God's Word. Asaph, who wrote many of the Psalms, thirsted for answers in his questioning of God in the seventy-third psalm.

- When he saw the wicked prospering, he cried out to God to understand why. "When I pondered to understand this, it was troublesome in my sight" (Psalm 73:16 NASB).

- He found the Lord to be his strength and realized that he desired nothing but Him. "My flesh and my heart may fail, but God is the strength of my heart and my portion forever" (Psalm 73:26 NASB).

- If we find ourselves thirsty, we can follow Asaph's example and draw near to God. "But as for me, the nearness of God is my good; I have made the Lord GOD my refuge, that I may tell of all Your works" (Psalm 73:28 NASB).

By putting our trust in God, we will stop being thirsty. He will remove that desire from our worldly appetite. Drink of His water and you will be satisfied.

> When you have no helpers, see all your helpers in God. When you have many helpers, see God in all your helpers. When you have nothing but God, see all in God; when you have everything, see God in everything. Under all conditions, stay thy heart only on the Lord.
>
> —CHARLES HADDON SPURGEON

—∞∞—

PRAYER: Father God may I always thirst after Your righteousness. Both in water and in spirit—I want to be healthy in both. Let me look forward to the time when we can be together. Amen.

ACTION: Increase your water intake today.

REFLECTIONS

Who I Am in Christ

As many as received Him, to them He gave the right to become children of God, even to those who believe in His name.

JOHN 1:12 NASB

Who am I? This is a basic question we face in life. In reality there are two audiences that answer that question: First, others—and second, God. Man's opinion is short-lived and will soon fade away, but God's thoughts are eternal and will be everlasting.

Nothing is more freeing than agreeing with God about how He sees you and me. That's why it is so important to be in a daily study of God's Word. This exercise will offer us crucial understanding:

- we will know who God is
- we will know who we are in Him
- we will know what we have in Him
- we will know what we can do through Him

Day by day we are to live out who we are as new creations in Christ Jesus. The following alphabet is just the beginning of our relationship with God the Father, God the Son, and God the Holy Spirit.

Able to do all things (Philippians 4:13).

Becoming conformed to Christ (Romans 8:29).

Chosen (Colossians 3:12).

Delivered (2 Timothy 4:18).

Equipped (2 Timothy 3:17).

Filled with joy (John 17:13).

Guarded by God (2 Timothy 1:12).

Holy (Hebrews 10:10).

Instrument of righteousness (Romans 6:13).

Justified (1 Corinthians 6:11).

Known (2 Timothy 2:19).

Lacking no wisdom (James 1:5).

Made by Him (Psalm 100:3).

Never forsaken (Philippians 4:19).

Overcomer (1 John 5:4-5).

Partaker of grace (Philippians 1:7).

Qualified to share His inheritance (Colossians 1:12).

Receiver of the riches of God's grace (Ephesians 1:7).

Sealed by God with the Holy Spirit (Ephesians 1:13).

Transformed into His image (2 Corinthians 3:18).

Useful for His glory (Isaiah 43:7).

Valued (Matthew 6:26).

Walking in new life (Romans 6:4).

e**X**ample (Ephesians 5:2).

Yielded to God (Romans 6:13).

Zeal for God (Romans 10:2).[19]

Just think of all the value we have in Christ! His Word says I'm important and have worth in His eyes. No matter what man may think of me, I have eternal value:

- I am deeply loved.
- I am complete in Him.
- He made me special.
- He made me beautiful in His sight.

- I am pleasing to Him.
- I am forgiven in Him.
- He wants to have fellowship with me.

—~~~—

Prayer: Father God, no matter what I think of myself, Your Word tells me I'm more valuable than gold or silver. As I look into the mirror may I see Your face reflecting back to me. Thank You for loving me so much. Amen.

Action: Each day go through one of the ABCs of who you are and study the reference Scripture.

REFLECTIONS

Take Time to Rest

Come to me, all you who labor and are
heavy laden, and I will give you rest.
MATTHEW 11:28 NASB

I f you've ever gone to the Grand Canyon in Arizona, you have seen those burden-bearing donkeys that carry goods, people, and materials down to the canyon floor. They seem so small yet they carry such heavy loads that it's easy to feel sorry for these animals. As you look at their swaybacks, it doesn't seem like they can continue one more step. It's sort of like the pickup truck that's overloaded with sand and gravel. You know the springs are going to break at any minute.

The lips of the wise will protect them.

—PROVERBS 14:3

Jesus saw people that way—burdened and stressed, weighed down by the legalism and the legalistic demands the Pharisees had placed on them. No matter where they turned, some politician was telling them what to do or what not to do. Matthew 23:4 states:

For they tie up heavy burdens and lay them on men's shoulders,
but they themselves are unwilling to move them (NASB).

We don't need religion that becomes an unbearable burden. We need rest from the terrible burden that sin and hopelessness create. That's why Jesus came! He came to give rest. By lifting the weight of sin from our shoulders,

God opened the way for full and free living as He originally intended for us. To walk in obedience is never a burden—it's freedom.

It is also physically healthy to rest from the stresses of life. In order to live a long life, we must reduce the pressures in our lives. Prioritizing will help us cast off the hurry of today's technological age. Never in the history of mankind have we as people been under more pressure to perform. We are molded into thinking that we must have a perfect marriage, a perfect family, a perfect career, a perfect home. Because of this pressure, we will break if we don't relax. Jesus says to come unto Him and He will give us rest.

PRAYER: Father God, we don't know what life would be like if You weren't alongside us to ease our burden. You have given me such great relief. Thank You! Amen.

ACTION: Get at least eight hours' sleep every night.

REFLECTIONS

Fear Not

*I have called you by name; you are Mine! When you
pass through the waters, I will be with you. And through
the rivers, they will not overthrow you. When you walk
through the fire, you will not be scorched, nor will the
flame burn you. For I am the LORD your God.*

Isaiah 43:1-3 NASB

Notice that Isaiah says "when," not "if." Sooner or later, all of us will
go through deep troubles. If you aren't right at this moment, you
eventually will. Stand in line—your time will come. Since we live in
Southern California where real estate prices are over the top, this slowdown
in the housing market has affected many of our neighbors. We have a lot
of "For Sale" signs on the front lawns. Several families tried to refinance
and couldn't and they had the bank foreclose on them. We have several
families finding out a member of their family has cancer, another family
having a sudden death of a family member, another teenage driver received
a DUI driving ticket. On and on it goes. Our circle of friends is probably
not much different than yours. The odds are that we are all going to have
problems.

The question becomes, what are you going to do about it when it comes
upon you? My suggestion is don't wait until the shoe drops, but prepare
yourself by being in God's Word daily, have an effective prayer life, and
attach yourself to a good support group who can come alongside of you
when such events happen.

> We shall steer safely through every storm, so long as our heart is right, our intention fervent, our courage steadfast, and our trust fixed on God.
>
> —St. Francis of Sales

When we are young or when life is treating us so well, it is hard to think about the woes of life. They might happen to others, but surely not to me or my family. But if the Lord grants us an abundance of years, we will all experience the woe that troubles so many people. We will all:

- Pass through deep waters.
- Wade through the rivers.
- Walk through the fire.

When these events of life happen I find that:

- God is always with me.
- The rivers aren't sweeping over me.
- The fires aren't burning me.
- God is calling me by name, and I will fear no evil.

—⁓—

PRAYER: Father God, let me turn my fear into faith. When I better understand that You have all my cares in Your care, I will be able to fear not. Amen.

ACTION: Prepare yourself to be able to withstand the storms of life. Have a plan.

REFLECTIONS

Comfort in Bad Times

I have learned the secret of contentment in every situa-
tion...for I can do everything God asks me to with the
help of Christ who gives me the strength and power.
PHILIPPIANS 4:12-13 TLB

My balloon popped and my world came crashing down when I first heard the words describing Emilie's illness, "You have cancer!" Why are we so surprised when life is difficult? In America we think that everything should be perfect: our marriage, our children, our government, our health, etc. Jesus told us life would be difficult and troublesome. However, so many think they're entitled to a trouble-free life—nothing but happiness, fun, and financial success. Then, when trouble inevitably comes, they're devastated. I have learned to expect the problems and let them teach me something... such as what's really important in life.

Through this long bout of discomfort, Emilie and I have had a lot more time to ponder just that. The little things that are free have gone up in our value system—a baby's hug, a sea breeze, a call from a friend, an afternoon jog on the beach. Big issues, such as money, prestige, and the stock portfolio, have gone way down the list.

> When one door of happiness closes another opens; but often we
> look so long at the closed door that we do not see the one which
> has been opened for us.
>
> —HELEN KELLER

Best of all, we're learning it's possible to feel content and peaceful even while bad things are happening—because we know it's all temporary. I can expect pain and trouble because that's part of living in the world, but I can trust God's promise that He'll carry me through it all.

> Man is, properly speaking, based upon hope, he has no other possession but hope; this world of his is emphatically the place of hope.
>
> —Thomas Carlyle

Prayer: Father God, just as You told the waves of Galilee, "Quiet, be still," calm the waves in my soul. Still the waters; come to me and bring me peace. Amen.

Action: List three eternal blessings in your journal. Ponder each one, write down your response, and let them help you be contented.

Reflections

Humility—God's Characteristic

Clothe yourself with humility toward one another,
for God is opposed to the proud,
but gives grace to the humble.

1 PETER 5:5 NASB

As I walk past the Monday night football games on television, I witness all kinds of strange dances. Most of them occur after a player has scored a touchdown. I can't help but think that a person doing such antics hasn't learned the first step in being humble. I was taught as a young boy to let my skills do the talking and to act in a calm, reserved fashion. It's not just football players on Monday night. The world has gone wild with pride. It's all about me!

Humility is a fundamental character quality at the heart of every successful relationship. Those who exhibit great pride usually don't have strong interpersonal relationships.

Peter writes: "Clothe yourselves with humility toward one another, because God opposes the proud, but gives grace to the humble. Humble yourselves, therefore, under God's mighty hand, that He may lift you up in due time." In present-day management books we read about climbing the corporate ladder, upward mobility, self-assertion, moving on up. It's always up. However, God seems to have a different program. The way up with God is always down. Peter's exhortation to be "clothed with humility" is a command, not a mere suggestion. God opposes the proud. The moment we allow pride to raise its ugly head, the resistance of God begins.

God not only resists and opposes the proud, He is clear in His teachings that the proud will be humbled.

A man's pride brings him low.

—PROVERBS 29:23

Paul teaches us this truth: When you are clothed with humility, God terminates His resistance against you. As God's children, we should be smart enough to stay on the good side of God by staying on the side of humility.

God always opposes the proud, yet if we are humble He will exalt us at the proper time.

- "Humility comes before honor" (Proverbs 15:33).
- "Humble yourself before the Lord and He will lift you up" (James 4:10).
- "He has brought down the rulers from their thrones, but has lifted up the humble" (Luke 1:52).

Then what is humility?

- It is moral realism, the result of a fresh revelation of God.
- It is esteeming others as better than ourselves.
- It is the fruit of repentance.
- It is the attitude which rejoices in the success of others.
- It is the freedom from having to be right.
- It is the foundation of unity.
- It is the mark of authenticity.
- It is the fruit of brokenness.
- It is the quality which catches the attention of God.

The end result is holiness. Our only response to God's holiness, and that of His Son, Jesus, is humility. If you are interested in developing a long-term relationship with God and others, make humility your goal. As we kneel at the feet of our Lord, He will lift us up.

Prayer: Father God, I so want to be a humble man in all that I say and do. Please make me aware of any pride in my life. Amen.

Action: Ask a close friend to check and hold you accountable for being humble in your Christian walk.

Reflections

Make Today Special

*Blessed are those who have learned to acclaim you, who
walk in the light of your presence, O LORD.*
PSALM 89:15

It's your choice. Today is not just an ordinary day. It's one like no other day we have ever lived. "This is the day the LORD has made; let us rejoice and be glad in it" (Psalm 118:24 NASB). No matter if it's raining, snowing, blowing, or roasting, we need to rejoice and be glad in this today. Let's do something special, make it fun. Let the wife and children wonder what's new with Dad. Stroll through the park, fly a kite with the children, rent a good family movie, clean out your closet, take the family out for ice cream.

Today is not an ordinary day. God has opened new opportunities; the past is history and tomorrow is not here. Today is all we can live, so let's celebrate. Let's read a book, write a poem, sing a song. God delights in showering us with His very special blessings. "Every good and perfect gift is from above, coming down from the Father of the heavenly lights, who does not change like shifting shadows" (James 1:17 NASB).

> The lure of the distant and the difficult is deceptive. The great opportunity is where you are.
>
> —JOHN BURROUGHS

Today is special because we realize that God freely offers us His best gifts to enjoy. In John 10:10 Jesus states, "I have come that they may have life, and have it to the full" (NASB). God wants us to have a full and abundant life. He has prepared a banquet table for us.

Because you are making this a special day, let's thank God for this free gift of life. Let's praise Him for who He is. Let's trust Him for the days to come. This abundant life fills the God-void in man's life and it also provides us with power to overcome the problems of life. So step out in faith and give Jesus all your cares.

> I shall be telling this with a sigh
> Somewhere ages and ages hence;
> Two roads diverged in a wood, and I,
> I took the one less traveled by—
> And that has made all the difference.
>
> —Robert Frost

Prayer: Father God, let me rejoice in this day that You have given to me. I want to count my blessings. Let me look at today as a gift from You. Amen.

Action: Discuss around the evening dinner table this question: "Why was today so special?"

Reflections

Notes

1. Kay Arthur newsletter. Used by permission of Precept Ministries.

2. Bob and Emilie Barnes, *Minute Meditations on Prayer* (Eugene, OR: Harvest House Publishers, 2003), pp. 13-14.

3. Robert J. Morgan, *Then Sings My Soul* (Nashville, TN: Thomas Nelson Publishers, 2003), p. 151.

4. Hyatt Moore, Wycliffe Bible Translators (Huntington Beach, CA: March 1995), adapted from a newsletter.

5. Adapted from Aesop.

6. Jennifer Rothschild, *Self Talk, Soul Talk* (Eugene, OR: Harvest House Publishers, 2007), pp. 177-78.

7. No information given.

8. Source unknown.

9. Bob and Emilie Barnes, *15 Minute Devotions for Couples* (Eugene, OR: Harvest House Publishers, 1995), pp. 17-19.

10. Sam Walton, *Sam Walton, Made in America* (New York: Doubleday, 1992), pp. 246-49.

11. Adapted from Dave Branin, *Our Daily Bread,* September 5, 2005.

12. Source unknown. Taken from an e-mail.

13. Inspired by a news bulletin from Carol Harrison (*Faith, Flowers, and Friendship*).

14. Source unknown. Taken from an e-mail.

15. Emilie Barnes, Kay Arthur, Donna Otto, *Youniquely Woman* (Eugene, OR: Harvest House Publishers, 2008), pp. 171-72.

16. *God's Little Devotional Book for Dads* (Tulsa, OK: Honor Books, Inc., 1995), p. 59.

17. Dennis and Barbara Rainey, *Building Your Mate's Self-Esteem* (San Bernardino, CA: Here's Life Publishers, 1986), pp. 56-57.

18. Source unknown. Taken from the Internet.

19. Author unknown.

Other Books by Bob Barnes

MEN UNDER CONSTRUCTION
Bob Barnes brings great insight to male readers looking for that special jumpstart to their day.

In this collection of timely readings, Bob offers practical insight in

- learning to communicate with his wife
- longterm commitment to God's plan for his life
- pursuing honesty and integrity in all his endeavors
- being the involved dad his kids need
- making the most of all God has given him

Here are devotions that will bring every man closer to God...and closer to those who love him.

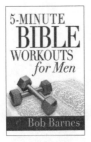

5-MINUTE BIBLE WORKOUTS FOR MEN
Bestselling author Bob Barnes provides a gathering of brief, powerful meditations, packed with encouragement, to help men handle daily pressures of family, work, relationships, and responsibilities. These devotions provide

- encouragement for busy lives and difficult times
- guidance to shape a man's character
- illustrations of how to serve, lead, and grow
- Scriptures for strength and wisdom
- prayers to connect with the heavenly Father

This spiritual workout will help men maximize their time with God and live out their faith through actions, words, and behaviors that honor Him.

For more information regarding speaking
engagements and additional material, please
send a self-addressed stamped envelope to:

More Hours in My Day
2150 Whitestone Drive
Riverside, CA 92506